NEVER HAD IT SO GOOD

NEVER HAD IT SO GOOD

by

JEAN COLIN

LONDON
VICTOR GOLLANCZ LTD
1974

© VICTOR GOLLANCZ LTD 1974
ISBN 0 575 01692 2

The lines by Kipling quoted on page 62 are from "The Female of the Species" and are reprinted from *The Years Between* by kind permission of Mrs George Bambridge and Macmillan & Co Ltd of London and Basingstoke and Macmillan Coy of Canada.

MADE AND PRINTED IN GREAT BRITAIN BY
THE GARDEN CITY PRESS LIMITED
LETCHWORTH, HERTFORDSHIRE SG6 1JS

For my children

CONTENTS

THE BEGINNING

Is there, for honest poverty,
That hangs his head and a' that?
The coward-slave, we pass him by
We dare be poor for a' that!
—BURNS

I SEE NOW that someone should have given me a book of rules. But they didn't, and after the collapse of my marriage I found myself penniless, jobless, with three children to support and, in time, the magnificent sum of £400, a sort of redundancy pay from my sixteen years of marriage. The only reason I had that was because the house was in our joint names.

There are plenty of books of rules, but they all tell you how to make your marriage work, never how to get along when it doesn't. In theory—and I came up against so many theories—there is always a vague someone or something to take care of you. A husband has to pay to his wife, that's the law, unless he disappears, or takes a lower paid job, or spends all his money on his next wife, or becomes ill. If and when the husband doesn't pay, and you can't find a job, then you can live on Social Security.

In theory you are supposed to stay with your husband for the children's sake. In reality children suffer very much when parents quarrel. In theory parents shouldn't quarrel, and there is a happy ending and love lasts forever. In reality you are left clutching a few blasted dreams and you take the children home to mother. Nothing is black and white any longer, just grey shot with purple.

You're on your own, which can be frightening, but refuse to talk about a sense of failure because you don't happen to conform to Society's laws. You still have a touching belief that everything is so nice really.

After ten years of hammer blows, descending from every

place that could possibly drop them, you are still unbowed, a trifle bloody maybe, yet still refusing to bend the head in shame. *But, by God, doesn't everyone try to make you.*

The comfortable laws of nice people don't apply to the poor. You have to forget all of them and learn again the law of the jungle, for at the bottom there is no pity, not even from the rest of the poor. You have to fight and fight and fight. You spend so much energy in this fighting, there is no time left for gracious living, as you wrestle with small officials who represent Society, the great They who wield authority over your life, and who in the end win.

Or do they? You say to Society, you can humiliate me because I am poor, you can take from me the little that I have, you can break my home, rob me of my children, maybe you have the right. Just don't expect me to forgive you. You cannot control my feelings—that right at least I shall claim; when I have nothing left at all, still I will defy you in my heart, and my bitterness will be passed on to my children and my children's children unto the third and fourth generation.

And because of this, in the end Society will lose.

My parents were happily married for over fifty years and I was their only child. They were ordinary working-class people, and their life was one long austere battle of making ends meet. They were intelligent, well-read and respectable; our library consisted of cheap reprints of the classics which must have been popular in the twenties, so I read Tolstoy and Dumas side by side with *The Fourth Form of St Kilda's.* Both parents left school at eleven, for there were no scholarships in those pre-1914 days, or if there were few parents could afford to take them up. My mother had been taught in school to curtsey to the squire and vicar, and some of this forced deference stayed with her to the end of her days, though she voted Labour secretly and taught me about suffragettes. My father, of Scottish descent, thought he was as good as anyone and bowed his head to no man.

There had been no divorce in my family. True, my paternal grandfather had three wives, as wives in Victorian times had a habit of dying young. My maternal grandmother had eight children and no money and was an old woman at forty. Her father had been a local preacher (chapel) but he couldn't read or write. He said his word was his bond so he didn't need to write, and people came to hear him from miles around. He was violently anti-Church, and "he'd turn in his grave if he knew you'd married a man who was a church-goer", said a relative to my mother.

As a child I was sent to church regularly and had a stable home and a good upbringing. We were hard up in the thirties with Dad on short-time and Mother working, but there was always a clean cloth on the table and we never ate fish and chips. My parents' careful, prudent habits were taught to me. Waste not, want not.

I cannot say very much about my husband's upbringing as he came from another country and I never saw his family. But they wrote, when after the war they could be traced, and they seemed very much the same as my own, careful, hardworking people, farmers, who lost their all in the war and were moved across the country. In theory there is no reason why our marriage should not have worked. But I can swear on my heart that if we'd remained together so that the state would not have to finance us, the children would not have been happy. Otherwise I'd have stayed.

The details of the whys and wherefores of my marriage break-up are too long to go into here, or perhaps anywhere. Incompatibility is a big word, stretching over many years of difference which would never have been bridged. Suffice it to say that we married at a time when to live for today was all. He volunteered for war from Argentine, a neutral country, to fight for his own country, which was subsequently lost to a dictator; this caused him much bitterness. I lived in a town where every night houses were bombed to hell around me and civilians were killed. We seemed to be on a great wheel that spun us round without thought or pity, and we grabbed at anything that might seem to be stability and never was. We made a land fit for heroes to live in, he and I, for I worked daily in an aircraft factory office and nightly in the National Fire Service; now I find I have to be a heroine to live in the peace.

After marriage we were far better off than my parents had been, for the war brought prosperity to Hicktown. We paid a deposit on a semi-detached suburban house with a garage and a big garden. We had a car.

We had then been married eight years, and had lived together for odd spells during that time. Mervyn was born in

1945, and the next year my husband was sent back to Argentine. I joined him a year later. But he found things had changed there, and it was difficult for foreigners to progress in jobs unless they were naturalised. Babies, of course, took Argentinian nationality, so when Kay was on the way we decided to return to England. I was now British again (I had lost my nationality on marrying a foreigner), and with my new passport I came back just in time for Kay to be born, while husband had to wait months longer for an entry visa.

He arrived, and found the same conditions here, and to me it was a little shattering to find him glorified in the war but rejected in the peace. He fought for freedom and in the end had nothing. He was not allowed by the trades unions to take any job until he was naturalised, was not allowed a council house or a licence to build for the same reason. After naturalisation he was pushed into a job as a mining fitter, on the understanding that in the event of unemployment he would be the first to go. Some of his countrymen are now, thirty years later, still living in hostels. He didn't particularly like England, and thought the English working-classes downtrodden.

We lived in rooms, and at Mother's, and waited for a licence to build a house, and when it was finally granted to us it was already too late.

"Nor is it my experience that people shed their marriages lightly," writes a lawyer, Bill Mortlock, in *The Inside of Divorce**. "Very much to the contrary. I have sometimes been appalled by the things people have to put up with to sustain them . . . I have not found, on the whole, that people come easily to divorce."

I didn't want to leave my nice house. But the charge was cruelty, and I could not wait the long years before a judge could grant—or not grant—a decree. The children were suffering. I saw a lawyer, and he advised me to leave.

Kay, my only daughter, was ten by now. A pretty tomboy of a child, loving animals and games, her outgoing exterior hid a tender, sensitive spirit. Kay faced the world boldly and cried in secret in her bedroom. She was intelligent, though not too fond of school work. She had a talent for ballet dancing, and when the compulsory lessons at her private school showed that she was above average I had paid for extra

* Constable (1972).

training out of the housekeeping money, and she passed all her exams with honours.

Philly, two and a half years younger, was a fair-haired, clever child with quiet ways and long deep thoughts. "Hasn't he a lovely smile?" gushed his junior school-mistress, and I feared that many women would be echoing her words in the years to come. Phil was no trouble.

Gentle Mervyn was fourteen, and the eldest. He loved poetry and beauty and thought on things that were lovely. Because he was handicapped he filled me with maternal battling feelings that were almost tigerish. I had to do much battling for Mervyn in the world, because the world isn't kind to handicapped people. As a child he was bullied, as an adolescent he was refused the right to work. He never complained.

My parents were living in a small terraced house with one room downstairs, a tiny kitchen, and a scullery containing a bath with a lid on top. No hot water, but a copper to heat up when required. One large bedroom and two small ones. No mod. cons. My father, after working for fifty-seven years in a job he hated, was hoping to spend his retirement in tending his garden and the roses he loved so much. My cheerful mother liked to entertain friends in the sitting-room. Both looked forward to ending their days in peace and quiet.

They didn't really want to take in a daughter, three children and a dog. But neither would they have seen us without a home. So one summer day in 1959, when I knew it would be impossible to go on any longer, we moved in. My marriage was ended.

2

EMPLOYMENT

No man is born into the world, whose work
Is not born with him : there is always work
And tools to work withal, for those who will :
And blessèd are the horny hands of toil!
—LOWELL

MY FIRST PRESSING need was for money. Husband
started sending £4 8s. od. for the children (30s. each less 2s.
postage); he had made it quite clear he would never pay anything to me if I should dare to leave my lord and master. I
was living rent-free at my parents' house, and it did not, at
that time, even occur to me to apply for National Assistance.
I should have felt this degrading. I had to find a job.

I hadn't worried too much about job prospects. I was a
trained shorthand-typist, and although my shorthand was
undeniably rusty I was, I thought, reasonably intelligent. I set
out confidently.

At my first interview I faced an elderly man who looked me
over shrewdly and asked my age. "Thirty-eight," I replied,
truthfully.

"H'm." He considered this, and so did I. Thirty-eight,
approaching forty. He asked, "When was your last employment?"

"Fifteen years ago," I said.

He looked glum. "Then you haven't worked for fifteen
years?"

I thought of the washing, the ironing, the cooking, the
cleaning, the mending, the nursing of children, the shopping,
the twenty-four-hours-a-day routine seven days a week. Not
worked? I said, "I was a housewife."

"Yes, quite." Apologetically, he went on, "I'm sorry, you
see, but you haven't worked for such a long time . . ."

"You think I've forgotten?" I asked.

"Well, yes," he said, relieved. "I'm sorry, Mrs—er—"

"That's all right," I said airily—I could afford to laugh—and hurried off to another appointment.

The second man said, "But you haven't worked for fifteen years."

I said, "No."

He asked, "Do you have any children?"

I hesitated. "My mother will look after them," I told him.

"Yes, but when they are ill—" In seconds I was being ushered out of that door too.

I called at the labour exchange. They said that they hadn't any jobs, and I couldn't get any unemployment benefit because I hadn't worked for fifteen years. I had no insurance stamps.

I wondered if I ought to start a protest meeting. Insurance stamps for married women. Paid by husband just as if she were a housekeeper. Just as if she *worked*. I decided to look into the matter of women's rights (married).

I couldn't find any, at least none worth mentioning. A married woman's status is based on the Case Law of 1660—"doint maintaine lour femmes ove necessaries . . ." She is a legal dependent, with rights to bed and board, the board in return for the bed, of course, for if she commits adultery there is no more board. If husband deserts the bed he is still supposed to maintain her, but for this she must apply to the magistrate's court, who may grant her an order, which husband may not pay. He can just disappear, or, if found, be sent to prison; either way there is no maintenance, which can come a bit hard if she has lots of tiny feet pattering around, resulting from the bed and board. And together with this serf status she cannot choose her own domicile, and has her social insurance and old age pension rights linked to husband's contributions.

But all this academic research didn't help me to get a job. I started out again.

It was a lovely summer. Hicktown's streets shimmered in a heat-wave, and they made my flimsy sandals extremely uncomfortable. I began to have the most amazing interviews, and applied for the most amazing jobs.

There was the little factory—I never did find out what it made—which was a scruffy place in a back street, with about a dozen workers altogether. The vacancy was for an operator to put a card on a machine, press a pedal and take the card out. The pay was £4 a week.

I went into a tiny office and the interview began. We went through the usual routine of age, qualifications, and the fact that I had not worked for fifteen years because I had three children. Said the man, "How much does your husband earn?"

This was a new one, and I pondered whether to tell a lie. I was already losing my shining honesty if not my purity (I hadn't been asked about that yet). I finally said I was separated, waiting for a divorce.

Perhaps that wasn't the right answer. Perhaps the wage was so low that I should have needed a husband with a fat pay packet to subsidise my earnings. I didn't get that job, either, and my morale sank into my flimsy sandals.

I applied for a job as a book-keeper. This was in another tiny office in a tumbledown building also in a back street. "Have you any experience?" asked the man behind the desk.

"Yes," I said, and it was true up to a point. I had done a teeny weeny bit of book-keeping once. I didn't think it necessary to tell him how many years ago.

"Up to trial balance standard?" he asked.

"Yes." I had no idea what trial balance was. So he asked me. And I guessed.

This employer was a canny Scot. "Funny sort of book-keeping you've been doing," he said, and we parted.

I applied for yet another job, and was called for interview. I kept getting these interviews because I wrote marvellous letters of application, implying that my knowledge was next to God's, and omitting all mention of any gaps in my employment because of marriage and children. But the question would arise: what have you been doing for the last fifteen years? Working? Prove it.

I thought I had solved the problem when I rooted out a man I used to work with during the war, and persuaded him to write me a reference as though he had been the boss and sign it with the current date. I took this confidently to the next interview, only to be told, "I never read references, they may be forged."

The children began to pester me about when I was going to start work. It didn't worry them in the least that they might, in the future, have to be latch-key children; they just wanted to eat regularly as their friends did. They saw Daddy,

with a fine simplicity, as the money provider. Without him
there was no cash, so Mum had to go to work. Children are
very practical. So practical that Philly thought it might be
a good idea to find another daddy-provider—anyone would
do. To this end he raked around acquaintances and even
perfect strangers, shouting, when any male under a hundred
passed by, "How about this one, Mum?", and I had to re-
strain him forcibly from asking to see the man's bankbook.
Even the fact that he was accompanied by a wife and five
children didn't deter Phil, who thus anticipated the Divorce
Reform Bill by some ten years.

It is, I know, generally given out that a child misses his
father very much. Perhaps it is not always realised that the
working-class child (I use this term for want of a better) has
an entirely different outlook and way of life from those who
are most interested in child welfare, and who are involved in
putting into operation schemes which are basically middle-
class. Your working-class child often sees very little of his
father. Dad is usually at work, doing overtime or shift or
night work, or being a long-distance lorry driver, or just
doing extra part-time painting and decorating for people. He
is seldom at home, and more often than not the child prefers
him to be out anyway. So does mother. Your working-class
wife really does work hard (perhaps the term is apt after all);
she often has a full-time job, does a terrific amount of housework, and looks after children and husband. She cannot
stand having "him" under her feet all the time. And, of course,
most working men in the Midlands and North think the kids
are women's work anyway.

The working-class child has more of a community life.
Usually he has relatives round the corner, and the street is his
playground. The street is part of working-class life, part of the
child's community; here he meets his friends, here he spends
many happy hours. (I am not talking of cities where there is
a traffic problem.) His mother stops to talk to neighbours, and
old people love to "watch the folks". One of the memories of
my childhood is of old men and women sitting in chairs outside their front doors, nodding to passers-by, talking to the
children. It's a continuation of the village green. And while
we have one group of experts busily trying to break up the
community life—keep children off the streets—a more
advanced guard is aiming to bring it back.

But working-class dad is often a shadowy figure, and although I have known one child ask his mother not to leave her husband when they had been having difficulties, I have known a great many more who begged to be taken away. In my mother's generation a bad-tempered husband usually got his come-uppance when the sons grew up and gave him a good hiding; this rough justice was meted out not so much because they were sorry for their mother's beatings as because they were angry about their own. If there cannot be two mistresses in one kitchen, it's for sure there cannot be two male bosses in one small home. Of course, life was rough in those days, and there was far more violence than today, but no one took any notice.

We were still living with my parents, and it wasn't too easy. Three generations in such a confined space meant there was bound to be friction. There just wasn't room. Somehow I had to find another place to live, but first I must get a job. There was also the question of Kay's school fees coming up.

Kay had been sent to this school because my husband and I—who were on speaking terms then—thought we'd make a little lady of her. And because, to be honest, all her friends went there, for we'd been living in one of the better suburbs of Hicktown, we were the up and coming of the Age of the Common Man. And finally, for the same reason that anyone sends their children to private schools rather than secondary modern; employers, and all those who help you to Get On in the World, prefer a snobbish background. (This paid off in later years.) Mervyn passed for grammar school but his poor health meant that he lost much time. Phil was still at junior school and doing well. (Phil always did, he had a convenient gift for falling on his feet.)

Kay's friends, unfortunately, all seemed to have lots of money, and this put us at a disadvantage. It's not so bad being poor in a slump when everyone's poor, but when everyone else is affluent you just get complexes. So Kay and Philly —who genuinely worried about money—kept up this barrage of, "When are you going to get a job, Mummy?" Maybe they felt insecure. We were insecure.

I made more frenzied sorties into the town. But Hicktown is not very large : it is, in fact, just a small Midlands industrial town exactly the same as the next Midlands town. It does not have the amenities of cities, but it doesn't have the problems either; there are no slums—the council was removing them in the thirties—and families who lived in basements were put into council houses and are now, a generation later, house-owners, or with small businesses, and getting along fine.

But there is not much in the way of employment in small towns, so I decided to seek further afield. Going to other towns meant spending lots on bus fares, and everywhere there were too many women chasing too few jobs, and the bosses always picked young girls, with no ties.

I tried a factory in Trimtown, where machinists were wanted. Anyone can use a sewing machine, and I *could*. I filled in a long form about all I had been doing since birth, and they turned me down. I got up one morning early to try for two hours' morning work at a jam factory, but the queue was so long I was too late at seven o'clock. I went to shops; one department store not only wanted to know my life story but if any relatives of mine worked there. Not knowing the right answer I wrote, "Yes", and was told by a friend later it should have been "No". Day after day I came home worried and a little scared, and told the children that I'd just been for a walk and everything was fine and I'd start looking for a job soon and then we'd all have money.

At last I found something. By now the last shreds of my shining honesty had departed and I was so desperate that I'd have told any tale if only I knew the right tale to tell. But this employer, of a transport firm in Trimtown, was desperate too, for oddly enough he couldn't get anyone to stay there. (No wonder, but I found that out later.) He told me he wanted a shorthand typist. Could I do that?

Anticipating a test, I babbled. "My shorthand isn't too good, but I don't need it, I can write so quickly that I can take down at any speed." He said he paid less than other employers. "That doesn't matter," I said. "Give me a trial, *please*." And I sat down, willing him to accept me.

These were the days before "work-ins", but I was determined to stay there in that chair till I had the job. I wouldn't have minded altogether if I'd had to pay him, so long as I had an insurance stamp and experience. He gave in. He told me to start on Monday. I was at work.

I had to enter through the garage, and the whole place reeked of petrol. I had a small office of my own, being the shorthand typist, and the girl who had worked there before me hadn't done any filing since 1924 or so. For days I sorted mounds of paper, and in between took dictation.

My office was reasonably quiet, the general office, where everyone else worked, was noisy, so the boss, in the cussed way bosses have, called me into the general office. There were three phones in this fairly small room, all ringing together, seldom stopping. There were drivers coming in and out asking about their routes, their pay, their hours lost last week, and explaining why they were five minutes late on a hundred-mile run. There were six clerks, one of whom was stone deaf to add to the fun, and three men who ran in and out of another office next door. I took dictation while the boss answered two phones and kept up a running conversation with six men and four clerks, leaving me to sort out what had been said. Usually I hadn't a clue.

But I wrote some kind of letters, and the boss always left the signing till closing time, which meant that I missed one of my buses—I had to get two. He was a meanie, that boss.

The remaining female staff consisted of two young girls, quite pleasant, and Lou, who worked the switchboard. When Lou was absent I had to take over, and I loathed and feared this job, for I could never hear a word owing to the general din, and things were further complicated by the fact that all the firms we dealt with had names like Telywastylir and Mestilluringo, or at least that's what I wrote down after asking them ten times to repeat.

I earned £7 a week and thought this was marvellous. True, I had to spend a lot on bus fares, and I was away from home a long time. But, being employed, I found it quite easy to find another job.

This was in an office nearer home and paid £1 less, but it meant that I was on hand to look after the children. The building was tall and grey, and had in fact been a boarding house until quite recently. My office was on the second floor, a large room, with a small gas fire heating one corner of it. My desk was next to the window, where I sat all alone watching the world go by like the Lady of Shalott.

In the next office was Bob, my boss, a nice young man, very pleasant and Boy-Scoutish. I was called a secretary, which sounded grand, but in the main I typed invoices. I never did any letters, as I don't think we ever wrote to any-one. There was a small switchboard on my desk, the bane of my life, for try as I would I could not work this miracle of our mechanised age. I knew vaguely that I had to press down two knobs and turn a little handle like a hurdy-gurdy, but whoever I tried to call, or whoever I tried to put through to Bob, I always got the men downstairs. So in the end I switched it through to Bob and let him take all the calls. He didn't mind.

I typed invoices, pages of them, reams of them. There were so many that I never had time to get them ready for posting. I always took piles home, where the children put them in envelopes and stuck on millions of stamps. They quite enjoyed it.

I was alone in the office, but there were many visitors. Reps on their way to see Bob, the men from downstairs popping in for a little chat, the cleaning woman, and one of the managers who called twice a week. He spent two hours with us, all of this with me, and most of it chasing me round the table. Luckily I was pretty nimble after all the exercise I'd had running after jobs. This game of catch-me-if-you-can started when I told him I was living apart from my husband. In time I learned never to tell a man this, for he reacts in one of two ways. Either he backs away in fear that you are about to drag him to the floor, or he tries to drag you on the floor. When the manager first sat down and asked what my husband did I said politely that I was separated. He didn't look like a wolf. He was about sixty, not what I would have called a greatly sexy type. But once he learned that I was on my own, he tried to help me keep my health and temper by informing me that if women didn't have sex *all the time*, when the menopause came they went mad. He offered me expensive presents and I refused to take a thing, like the pure heroine of an old romance. Well, we each have our own methods of barter; some of us demand a wedding ring for the bed, others prefer diamonds and an expensive flat. I might have settled for the latter myself—after all, I had had one wedding ring, and much good it did me. Looking back, and if I knew as much then as I know now, I would have started then and there on the primrose path; then I shouldn't have been poor and bitter, and my children would have been much better off. If there's a moral to this story it is that being good gets you nowhere, and the Victorian novels were wrong.

When the boss had gone the cleaning woman would creep up to my office and whisper, "What's happened, then?", and I'd tell her, and we'd sit and talk and go into peals of laughter, and I'd have to take the invoices home again.

Bob, dear innocent, didn't suspect anything. I don't remember why I told him. Perhaps I was just in a mood.

He stared. "Do you mean," he asked, "that he's been insulting you?" Bob was the picture of a good clean man, and that's what he was.

"I suppose so," I said, a little doubtfully. Which is worse, to have men chasing you, or not to have men chasing you?

"I'll have a word with him," said Bob the upright.

"Don't be a fool," I advised. "He's your boss. Why do you think I don't push him through the window? Because I wouldn't get a reference. And if you upset him you'd just lose your job. Neither you or I belong to any union, unfortunately. Remember what happened to old Bill."

Old Bill had an accident at work. The firm sacked him. He didn't get any compensation. He died. It's a hard world, the world of the poor.

So I looked for another job, sighing the while, for this one was convenient for many things, near my parents' home, having no stiff rules, so that Phil could come in and wait for me. I didn't mind too much about the boss, it was simply another annoyance when I had quite enough to cope with at home. I didn't really mind his insinuations about going mad; it was just that these things have a nasty habit of coming into your thoughts when you can't sleep, together with other bits of propaganda put out by psychiatrists, doctors, clergy and the writers of Auntie May's column, that without a father my children would grow up to have breakdowns, become homosexual, prostitutes, delinquents, etc. I agree with all of them that divorce isn't very nice, but can't we just leave it at that, so that I don't have to feel guilty all the time?

My next office had a woman supervisor and the pay was better, though the job was boring, copy typing *ad nauseam*. The office was clean and I shared with three other girls, of whom only one was having an affair with one of the bosses.

The children were happy. I paid Kay's fees, I gave them pocket-money, and Mervyn won a prize for a poem in a local festival of arts.

I started looking in earnest for a home of our own.

3

THE HOUSE

The stately homes of England,
How beautiful they stand.
Amidst their tall ancestral trees
O'er all the pleasant land.
—MRS HEMANS

I HAD BEEN searching for a long time for furnished accommodation, but even if I could have heard of two or three
rooms going cheaply no one would have accepted three children and a dog. My lawyer would have liked to claim the
marital home for us, and he wrote a nice letter to that effect,
but husband said not unless I could pay my half-share
cash down, and I could not, as he had all the money of the
marriage, while I'd been the little woman at home.

I went to the town hall and asked if I could have a council
house. "Ha ha," said the council house official jovially. "No,
of course not. We can't give houses haphazardly to every
woman who leaves her husband, can we? Ha ha."

"Ha ha," I echoed politely. "Why not? We are homeless."

"Do you know," his face had sobered, "that one council
did do such a thing, and was pulled up by the judge when the
woman's divorce case was heard for anticipating his judg-
ment? We could grant you a mortgage, if you wanted to buy
a house . . ."

I am still trying to figure out why it is anticipating the
judge's decision to rent a house to a woman, but not to sell
one to her. This must be one of the finer points of law I
can never understand.

There was nothing for it but to buy a house, I thought,
and I went to discuss the matter with my friend Mary and her
husband. I didn't seem to have many friends at that time;
after the break-up they seemed to drift away like autumn
leaves. I realised for the first time the loneliness of the odd
one out, perhaps felt more keenly by those who have been

part of a couple. Widows feel it, and widowers, and divorced men, and, I suppose, all the other odd ones who are not part of family life. It is only when you become an Odd One that you realise the full flood of propaganda which forms almost the whole of daily life. Happiness is a family, mother, father and children, and everything must fit this pattern rather than patterns fitting to people. I have been told since then by people alone, men as well as women, that the times they dread most are holidays—it isn't easy to get a single room. So life becomes a time when you only feel happy when working, and Christmas can be a nightmare. You don't get invitations any longer, not to share with *couples*, and you're afraid to go to your children's parent-teacher association annual dinner—or any other dinner for that matter—because you haven't a partner. And it's still not really done for a woman to go into a pub alone, in any class or area.

There is no one to confide in, and you have to pretend to the children that everything's fine, see how you're laughing. Each to her own image, and that of the divorcee is Madly Gay. Sometimes I wonder what would happen if the images were mixed up.

"I'll buy a house," I told the children, when they complained about lack of space. "No, it won't be where we lived before, I'm afraid, but I'll do the best I can."

The half-share of the money from the marital home, when the big mortgage had been paid off, worked out at about £400. I walked round Hicktown looking for a house I could afford. Hicktown is not very pretty, yet to some it is the place of their dreams. Many a loyal heart beats in its streets of terraced houses, many a staunch friend can be found in the few streets of better houses, and many a broken heart can be found in any area. Perronporth Road is a little apart and is where the nobs live, the nobs of Hicktown consisting of teachers, two or three doctors, a lawyer or two, and tradesmen who have made their pile.

Perronporth Road was out from the start. So were the nicer suburbs. There was nothing for us but something cheap, probably in one of the old streets in the centre of the town, leading to the open air market, that relic of ancient custom, where we'd get entangled with the fresh vegetables and meat and dust and cars trying to run down the throngs.

I saw a lot of cheap houses. Some, terraced, had back doors

about one yard away from their neighbours, with no bath and the lavatory down the garden. Some didn't smell very nice, some were grubby, some had old bedsteads sagging round the bit of garden-soil in place of a fence; none had any privacy.

Sometimes I went to the front door of these dwellings— as the estate agent called them, against the villas of Perron-porth Road—which usually opened on to the street. I would knock, knock again, and wait. After about half an hour some-one would open a window at the side and shout, "Come round the back, we can't open the front door, never opened it for years, and there's furniture/Dad's bike next to it."

So I went round the back, if I could find it. This often en-tailed walking another half-mile at least; going to the end of the street, walking into the next street, turning up a back alley, pitch dark, and finding out, by guesswork, which was the old gate leading to the house I wanted. I began to feel very sympathetic towards milkmen, who, oddly, always went to the backs of these dwellings but to the front of the Perron-porth villas. What class distinction lies here? I hadn't time to wonder; when I had opened two wrong gates, been snarled at by five surly dogs, fallen over an old bedstead/pram, I walked down the garden path into the tiny yard and found the door, only to be told the house was sold.

I applied to rent two shops, for I thought this might be a good way of combining business with a home. So widows of former times managed to eke a living by opening a shop in the front room of a house; the council won't allow it now.

The first was a small draper's. Mrs B. showed me round the living quarters, and they were grim. One room at the back, a couple of bedrooms with peeling plaster and a land-ing which seemed to be caving in. "We're always asking the landlord to repair it," said Mrs B., "but he never does." She mentioned his name, an honoured one in Hicktown, a trades-man who had not only made his pile but somehow gave the impression that he was charitable with it too. Mrs B. kindly warned me that the takings would not be enough to support a family, so I went on my way.

I tried another shop, owned by a small business man and at present being run by his daughter. "She's getting tired of it," said the lady who showed me over. "Her husband is a teacher, gets good pay, and they take other teachers as lodgers." We had reached the upstairs where the teachers lodged, and it was very cosy. "They're no trouble," the lady went on expansively. "They get their midday meal at school, and for tea we just give them some of the cold meat left over from the shop. They have a separate entrance as we never mention it to the income tax people."

I smiled. Of course, it's the done thing to diddle the income tax man. Respectable people do it. (That's why.) Perhaps crime depends on the status of the criminal, and if all the upper classes suddenly had to live on Social Security there'd be no more scroungers, just respectable pensioners. *See how yond justice rails upon yon simple thief . . . Change places, and handy-dandy, which is the justice, which is the thief?* as Shakespeare said. He knew all about mixed images.

I reckoned I'd be able to keep this place going and pay my way, with shop and boarders. But the man turned me down because I hadn't a husband. Not from any moralistic feeling, but because I'd have no money to fall back on. Business men, like children, are realists.

I kept on searching, and then I found IT.

Byfield Road consisted of houses on one side and a pit and old brickworks on the other, and the house was a bargain (or so I thought). It was going for £1,400 because the owner was desperate to get into the new home he'd built, and he dropped the price another £50 while I waited. So I agreed to buy, and then set about getting a mortgage. The Council's department were on holiday, but this didn't worry me for I had read that discrimination against women no longer existed in building societies.

I tried a leading society. "Well," they hedged, "we do lend to women, yes, but only to those who aren't likely to marry, you know, like school teachers." I didn't get the point, and said so. And how did they know whether the women school teachers would marry or not? But they wouldn't enlarge. I had the feeling that it was something to do with security and a safe job.

I tried another society. "Oh yes," they said, breezily. "We lend to women. We require a male guarantor, of course. Your father? He's over seventy? Sorry, no. Of course, if he would give us the deeds of his house as security . . ."

"And a merry Christmas to you, too," I said politely, as I made for the door.

I told my troubles to the house agents, and it was they who

finally fixed me up. Perhaps they were desperate to sell the old house too. Or perhaps they were genuinely kind. I wouldn't know, for I was getting to the point where I hardly recognised kindness.

"How much do you earn?" the agent asked, filling in the form.

"£6," I said.

"And how long have you been with the firm?"

"One week." I must say I was surprised when I had that mortgage.

It was a peculiar house, as though the builder kept changing his mind while he was building it. And as a matter of fact he did just that, the former owner told us. Thus, in the living-room there were two windows and a long beam running across the ceiling where he had been going to build a kitchen but decided against it. Instead he stuck the kitchen on at the back, with a tiny dark pantry joined on to it, and a coal-place and lavatory joined on to the pantry.

Although the living-room had two windows it was very dark, for the light from one was obscured by the kitchen/coalhouse/lavatory, and from the other by the neighbour's house, exactly three feet away. The front room was larger, with an old fashioned sash window which wouldn't open. (We found out later that none of the windows would open, and some had been nailed down.) The view was of the street and the coal mine dead opposite, complete with tip. It looked very well in the winter when it snowed, and we could imagine it was a mountain.

Upstairs, the front bedroom ran the whole width of the house. Then a queer little landing took us to two tiny rooms at the back, each with a fireplace, though with a bed inside there was no room to keep coal, let alone light a fire. The bathroom, with a squat little bath on legs, was over the hall. The boiler was, oddly, in the hall itself, a huge monster, looking as though it held a thousand gallons of water. Sometimes I wondered if that house was built with second-hand scraps.

We moved in, with the furniture we had salvaged from the marital home. This we had shared. My husband had the new bedroom furniture, the kitchen cabinet, all the curtains, the living-room furniture, the electric fire, all the garden tools and the car. I had two beds, the sewing machine, genuinely a hundred years old, one wardrobe, the piano, given to us by my mother, the bedroom furniture, given ditto, several odd chairs and a settee, a carpet, and a washing machine I had bought myself when I worked.

We laughed about the kitchen, which was a gem. This tiny fragment of architecture had three doors, a small window, a small sink, a space previously occupied by an old brick copper, and another space where stood the cooker included in the sale, which seemed about as ancient as the house. There was a soft-water tap, and I spent many hours wondering where the rain water tank was, for we turned on the tap and water came out all right. I began to think it must be piped straight up to heaven. Then one day it rained heavily and we discovered where the tank was. *Over the kitchen, in between the ceiling and the roof.* We found out, for when it rained the tank overflowed and dripped through the ceiling on to the floor. To this day I don't know how the rain got into the tank, but I would love to meet that builder.

I didn't dislike Byfield Road. The neighbours were pleasant, if a little close. We were, at the start, quite happy there. It was here that Gypsy came to join us.

Sandy, our last dog, had developed an unhappy habit of running to the nearby farm and slaughtering chickens. The first time the farmer caught him he was lenient, for he knew I was hard up. But on one side of the garden there was a low fence which blew down whenever there was a strong wind, and Sandy could just hop over and was away, up to the farm.

The second time the farmer was stern. "Get rid of that dog or I'll prosecute," he said. "Six of my best chickens dead." I knew that once started on the killing path Sandy would never reform, so one sad night I took him to the vet and walked home with an empty lead. Kay cried, Mervyn wrote a requiem, Philly was white and silent.

We missed Sandy. The house seemed like a morgue, with tears and dirges and reproachful looks coming my way. "Can't we have another puppy?" asked Kay.

"No more dogs," I said firmly. "Dogs are a luxury, they have to eat."

Then my friend Mary turned up and listened to our tale of woe. "Why not have a bitch?" she suggested. "They don't wander away as dogs do. And you could breed from it and make money. It would have to have a good pedigree, of course." I thought about it, and saw there was sense. Say, six puppies at £10 a time. Why, we could make a fortune. Well, make a bit to ease our stony path. At the very least the animal would pay for her keep.

That was the theory. But theories are not facts, and the plans of mice and men, and of women also, gang aft agley. Mine ganged too.

But the children were pleased. Within seconds Kay's tears stopped, the colour returned to Phil's cheeks, and Mervyn started an epic, "The Story of our New Dog."

I bought a copy of the *Dog World* and was surprised to learn how many kinds of dogs there were. I passed over Afghan hounds, they looked to have expensive tastes. We needed someone to rough it a little, some pedigree aristocrat who wouldn't be averse to eating off the floor, if necessary, or not to eat at all. I plodded through alsatians, boxers, great danes, dalmations . . . We didn't want a big dog, she'd eat too much. I came to scotties and halted. "A scottie should be ready to do anything and go anywhere," said the headline. Wasn't that what we wanted, for heaven's sake? Who knew what we might be doing or where we might be going this time next year?

And those little legs surely wouldn't be able to jump the fence. That settled it. A scottie it should be. Already I could see her in my mind's eye, a brave little animal, bright and intelligent, smart and good-tempered. I would name her Gypsy. I studied the names of the breeders and picked one at random. I drew £10 out of the bank, which left about £5, then caution returned.

"Look," I said, "I can't promise. I mean, it's a lot of money . . ."

There was a concerted howl, and Kay said stubbornly, "We need a puppy, all children do, I read it in a book."

Cursing the expert writers of advice to other people I took the train to see one Mrs Smith, a breeder of scotties.

Mrs Smith told me she had no small puppies, only two five-month-old bitches. I asked the price. "£15," she said.

I turned to run. "You can just see them," said Mrs Smith.

I said I would, to prove to the children that I had, and we went to the kennels.

One of the bitches was eager, bright-eyed, and ran to greet me wagging her tail cheerfully. The other stood in the back-ground. I had done my homework, I knew which was the better animal, the bright, cheerful tail-wagger. I turned to go again, then paused, staring at her sister, who looked at me pathetically.

I bent down to her. I always sympathise with the under-dog, and much good it does me. I wondered if she'd be left, unwanted, if someone would buy her who didn't care . . .

"Look here," said Mrs Smith, "I have to go into hospital shortly, I'm having to sell most of my animals. If you really want one of these you can have it for £5."

I stopped again, and the pathetic dark eyes gazed wist-fully at me. In five minutes' time she was under my arm and had become the new member of our family.

Expecting to bring back a small puppy—if anything—I had no lead. It was a long journey home, carrying a heavy dog. As at last I staggered along Byfield Road I saw the children's bedroom lights on. They were peering through the windows, and when I entered the house they ran downstairs with whoops of joy to see the new dog. Suddenly it all seemed worth while.

I put her on the floor and she stared around this house so strange to her, saw the settee and jumped on it, looking down. And there, metaphorically speaking, she stayed.

The next few weeks were spent in getting to know one another, or rather in our getting to know Gypsy, for she made no overtures, no halfway measures. She remained on the settee, and was most affronted if anyone else challenged her right to this. She would have no roughness, no shouting or even slight upbraiding. Anything in the way of a reproof made her turn her head away, deeply offended, and refuse to wag her tail for hours. It took much pleading on our part to get her in a good mood again.

She padded round the house like a little black teddy-bear and badly wanted to follow us upstairs. She made the effort gallantly, falling from top to bottom the first time. But she had typical Scottish persistence, and finally made it.

After that she wanted to come up at bedtime, too, and if we shut our doors would potter up and down stairs all night so that none of us could sleep. In the end one of us—me—would jump out of bed, drowsy and cold, and open the door.

She came to mean a lot to us, our shaggy scottie. If the world turned away its head, she was loyal. Stubborn, tough, not very bright, in her odd little way she loved us. And whatever came and went in the next ten years, even when the world crashed around me, I still had Gypsy . . .

It was in Byfield Road, too, that my children's lives set in the pattern which was to have far-reaching results; one was broken by society, one became a conformist through fear of it, and one determined to fight it.

We didn't know that then. It was spring, and Kay and I took Gypsy walking along the nearby heath, where wild roses grew in summer and blackberries in autumn. Blackberries are very useful things to have nearby, they make wonderful pies and are free. We tried a lot of free food while we lived there, including dandelion leaves and nettles, which the old folks say are excellent tonics. "I wonder," I said to Kay, "why we bother to plough and sow and all the rest of it when we can eat weeds gratis."

Kay was holding on to my arm, laughing at Gypsy. Mervyn was at home, working, for his handicap made him slow, and he sat patiently trying to work out those sums which never would come right, and copying out long pages of work he'd missed because he had been away ill. Philly had homework, too, for his junior school, but he skipped through it quickly.

Kay and I called on Mrs Carter, a dear old lady who lived further along the road. She was a widow and lived alone, though crippled with arthritis. Her son, who had a good job, had emigrated to New Zealand. An intelligent woman, she had been a leading light in the Co-op movement, and still did a lot of writing in a beautiful hand, even though she found it difficult to move her fingers.

In the Midlands and north the Co-ops played a leading part in the lives of intelligent working-class women. They would go to Women's Guild meetings—my mother did—and here they would sometimes study, enter for educational courses and so on, all, it seems, unknown to the great world outside. For many other women Co-ops just meant "divi", and when this was in their own name it was never paid out to husbands, even in the bad old days when husbands could claim everything of their wives'. Perhaps this was the beginning of women's liberation, this quiet sitting down of ordinary women to work for the betterment of their positions and, through them, of the world.

We gossiped, of course, and we learned about life in Byfield Road. About Mr A., who blacked his wife's eye every

time they went out together because he said she'd looked at
other men. Both Mr and Mrs A. were sixty, and he'd been
blacking her eyes all their married life.

The miners were earning good money at that time and
ran cars, had well-furnished houses, and had changed a great
deal since the bad old thirties. Yet for many of them the old
"eye-blacking" attitudes persisted. "I'm the boss and don't
you forget it," and "Have my dinner ready on the table when
I come home from the pit or I'll tip the table up." And they
did, too.

But the women were beginning to change *their* attitudes.
With prosperity they could afford it. "I'll get a job, then I
won't be dependent on his money," was the theme, and the
surprised "mester" found that his former slave was ready to
walk out and support herself. "Go, and I won't pay a penny
to you, I'll go to prison fust," the men threatened. And they
did that, too.

Not that the miners were terribly happy at work. Or perhaps it was just that they weren't as happy as they'd expected
to be. Back in the old days they'd had little money for hard
graft, and they'd thought that nationalising the mines—the
dream for so long—would be the answer. And somehow it
wasn't. They had more money, but they were uneasy. They
didn't like their new bosses. They grumbled because there
were so many of them—"ten men where there was one afore"
—they missed the old type gaffers, men who'd worked up
from the bottom, knew every inch of the pits and understood
the men's problems. Now they had the new élite, educated,
academic, smart young men, and the old miners despised and
distrusted them. The pits still didn't belong to the people.

Worst of all was the bureaucracy, which they could neither
understand nor fight. What did a thousand faraway faceless
ones know of their troubles? Whom could they see to complain to? There wasn't even anyone to hate these days.

So they brood to each other in the closed society of the
working class, from which emerges the shrewd and cynical,
mining, factory-working Midlands Man. His humour is harsh,
sardonic, and he doesn't talk to strangers. He goes to school
but learns history from his parents; about the men who dug
coal in the fields during the general strike; the dreaded Means
Test; grandads on the farm who stole turnips because their
families were starving; great-grandads in the pits who re-

* *

membered little boys being carried out because they were too exhausted to walk; weavers who hated Queen Victoria because her insistence on lengthy mourning put them out of work; factory owners who brought over cheap foreign labour to cut the wages; men who came back from the last war and said that this time there was going to be a change or else . . . He learns to distrust at his father's knee, and he drinks bitterness with his mother's milk. His eyes are watchful and wary, and his mouth is sullen. He votes Labour but doesn't believe in the brotherhood of man because he's never seen it in practice.

He never confides in his wife, or talks to her about his work; if he goes on strike she doesn't know why. (This is a pity, for she could be his greatest ally; it is why some women now urge their husbands to get back to work—they don't know what the dispute is all about.) He seldom tells her what he earns, and quite often gives her too little house-keeping money, for he can never quite see why he should support her.

But it would be unfair to say that the working class male is basically either selfish or brutal. Although, in the main, a rough job makes a rough man, I have known miners who were —and are—gentlemen, and husbands who nursed sick wives as gently as any woman, and did not lose caste thereby. But where men work in jobs requiring physical strength, then masculinity becomes a virtue admired by both men and women. Most working class wives don't want their husbands to help in the house; they expect him to be the boss. They prefer this, and the weak man is despised above all others. It is similar to the attitude all women adopt in war-time, when the male is the conquering hero. "I can't work out of town, my husband likes me to come home at dinner-time with him," said a factory worker to me recently, and in a young wife this is a boast. With the years attitudes change, and, "Marry for love the first time, marry for money the second," says the middle-aged housewife.

But the working class male never makes a pathetic spectacle of himself, in middle-age, by chasing young girls. (He might go after other women, but prefers his own age group.) He never, even in youth, goes much for the simpering, pretty-pretty type; the tomboyish girl who drinks with the boys is the one who gets married first. His wife must be

2—NHISG * *

strong, a worker, for he can't afford a status symbol. And even with the male domination there is a camaraderie among the sexes brought about by going to school together, playing and working together from childhood, that is possibly lacking in other circles.

We talked things over, Mrs Carter, Kay and I, and I thought about this dear old lady with her sweet ways and her backbone of steel. She had left school at eleven, yet she had educated herself, had travelled as a delegate for the Co-operative movement, and ensured that her own son bettered his lot, even though it meant that he went to another country and left her alone. She died soon afterwards, and went to her grave un-noticed by the big world. Just another ordinary woman.

Kay and I drifted back to our own house, where Mervyn was still struggling with his maths. He turned his perplexed face to me as I entered, but I couldn't help him—my education had ended at fourteen, and I wasn't up to that standard. I worried about Mervyn, but was sure he'd be all right; that something would be found for him in the future with all the new laws and provisions for the sick and handicapped.

I turned my attention to the pets we'd somehow picked up in the space of a few days. Besides Gypsy there was the goldfish, given to Kay by a friend, which was without exception the largest, ugliest goldfish I had ever seen; and the chinchilla, which we had salvaged from the marriage, and which had been bought because someone had told us they would breed lots of little chinchilla and make us a fortune.

They never did. In the end one died and we sold the other. But in the meantime we kept them in a cage in the empty back bedroom. Luckily no officials of the Health Department ever wanted to look round.

Chinchilla are nocturnal animals, so every night they would be clumping and thumping around in their room. In the morning the swallows would take over—they had a nest under the eaves of the other bedroom, and seemed to wear hob-nailed boots most of the time. There is something so very English and countrified about swallows. They came back every year and we watched for them eagerly.

Gypsy's puppies were born in the living-room, with the goldfish glaring from the bowl and the chinchilla banging away upstairs. I had taken Gypsy to meet her bridegroom.

Miss Lee was another well-known breeder, and when she looked at Gypsy she said, "Oh dear, she is shaggy." I frowned worriedly—Gypsy didn't like travelling, in fact, she didn't like doing anything. "Perk up, girl," I hissed. She looked unimpressed. I don't think I've ever seen an animal look so *uninterested* the whole time.

When she returned from her nuptials she looked more miserable than ever, and slightly baffled, as many a virgin before her has felt on her wedding night. Is this what all the fuss is about, for heaven's sake? I paid the fee and we departed.

In due course four healthy puppies were born. I had been up all night, hovering apprehensively around the mother-to-be, book of instructions in my hand. I had prepared a basket, but Gypsy ignored this and jumped on the settee. This was in keeping, at any rate.

After a first look of utter astonishment she began to lick the new arrivals into shape, while I went to tell the children, who ran downstairs quicker than ever in their lives. Gypsy lay, blankly impassive as ever. If she was proud she didn't show it. We had a celebration cup of tea and drank to the new arrivals, the Pedigree Pups, who were to be the first of a long line which would ultimately make our fortune.

We loved those pups. Kay loved them, as she loved all animals. Mervyn, the quiet and shy, loved them. But it was Philly, the self-contained, the quiet boy with the determined eyes who really let himself go about them, and for this child, at least, the pups brought happiness.

I sold them for a total of £30. Our town didn't much go in for pedigree dogs. And I'd had to pay the vet and the stud fee and buy good food. It was doubtful if Gypsy would make our fortune, but by this time she was one of us. We never could look on her as a *working* dog; we worked, Gypsy stayed an aristocrat.

In my spare time I was decorating. I was able to get perks from the office where I worked in the form of cheap piant and wallpaper from shops at a discount. I started with the living-room, the children helping me. They had to. We pulled the dirty old paper off the walls, and tried to get it off the ceiling, but found the ceiling came off too, so we just had to paint over it. A coat of nice white paint hides a multitude of sins. I painted most of the walls white, putting in a panel of paper in the centre. It was washable paper, in fact it was for bathrooms, with sea and boats and birds waving along in rows. I figured that if we couldn't go on a holiday we could look at the wallpaper. As a finishing touch I bought yellow venetian blinds for the windows, thinking they'd give the effect of sunlight as the books tell you. They never did, just looked like yellow venetian blinds.

I marched on with my triumphant progress into the front room, which in a dwelling is never a lounge. Lounges belong to the nesh and rarefied air of Perronporth Road. There was little to do here beyond painting the old firegrate white to make it look like one of those in a stately home.

The kitchen nearly defeated me. There was no paper here, or plaster even, just bare bricks which had been painted over and over again, and were now dark green to add to the general gloom. I bought some vinyl covering in a clean light blue and white. I stuck it on, and immediately it all dropped off. I made more paste and stuck it on again. This time it held, but whenever the kitchen got too hot the edges would begin to curl, so that our walls sometimes gave the effect of a fading rose.

The electric cooker had a wire winding round the room and coming to a dead stop in mid-air on one wall. I had taken no notice of this, nonchalantly cooking every day around it. Quite by chance I happened to mention it to Bob at the office. "Should I paper over it?" I asked.

His reaction was alarming. "Great Scott, that's dangerous. The wire should be earthed. You could easily be electrocuted. I'll come and fix it for you." Bob was a nice boss, and he made the cooker safe, though he couldn't do much about the light sockets hanging out of the walls. The house badly needed re-wiring.

Later I bought a cheap sink unit for about £4, and had the old sink taken out. It became quite a nice little kitchen, if you didn't mind working in a restricted space.

There was still the upstairs to renovate. I lay in the bed I shared with Kay and studied the cracks which criss-crossed the ceiling, and wondered what to do.

"We could," suggested Kay, "have tiles."

I rejected this. I saw blue patterned paper for the walls and a matching pattern for the ceiling. I bought rolls of each sort and we ate more nettles than usual that week. True, I had never papered a ceiling before, but there's a first time for everything.

The walls were easy, and the next evening—for this had to be done when I came home from the office—I looked at the long ceiling and felt a little bothered.

I took the table upstairs, and pulled a chest of drawers to the other end of the room. Then I walked the length of the table, jumped on the drawers and walked along them too, measuring the paper. All I had to do now was put it on.

I tried the same methods I used with the walls, smoothing it on with my hands. But if you've never tried to put an eight-yard length of paper on a ceiling, walking along a table and jumping on to a chest of drawers, you won't understand what I mean, and I doubt if anyone else in Britain has ever papered this way.

The first time I kept my eyes on my feet and put the paper on in a pretty curve facing east. The second time I kept my eyes on the ceiling and fell off the table. Sitting on the floor with the roll of paper round my neck I heard Kay ask, "Are you hurt?"

I extricated myself, whispering words I didn't even know I knew. "Let's try again," I said aloud, clamping my stiff upper lip in place.

I papered that ceiling, but I hope I may never do another. At the end my neck felt as though a sharp knife was stuck in between it and my head. I had to walk around for days with my eyes cast meekly down, like a nun. I ached everywhere.

Decorating the two tiny rooms was child's play after this. I even found a man to open the sash windows, though it was quite a job. Apart from the nails and paint which stuck them down, all the cords were broken.

Our one lavatory was outside in the yard, which meant that each morning, and when Mervyn was ill in bed, I had to take a bucket and empty slops. So I applied for a council grant which would pay half towards installing a lavatory and wash-basin in the bathroom, and I had an immersion heater put in the boiler and an airing cupboard built round it. I papered the bathroom, and had a board nailed along it to hide its funny squatness and tiny fat legs.

This made life a little easier for me, but I was really trying to make the house like the labour-saving semi I had lost. I didn't succeed.

4

THE DREAM COTTAGE

Dreams are but interludes which Fancy makes;
When monarch Reason sleeps, this mimic wakes.
—DRYDEN

AS THE FIRST winter on our own went by, I found more disadvantages in the old house. The garden was a long narrow strip, and the sagging fence on one side still blew down with sickening regularity. We nailed it up as best we could, for I could not afford a new one.

The winds brought other troubles too. The chimney was faulty; clouds of smoke would pour down into the room, but it was too cold to be without a fire, and if we lit the front room one we had no hot water, for two fires were out of the question.

Then the pipes began to freeze. They were placed, of course, in the most exposed niche of the kitchen, yards of them, all running down beside the window. Every frozen morning before I went to work I had to pour kettles of boiling water down those pipes.

The bath water refused to run away—obviously the waste pipe was frozen too. I went outside and poured boiling water round the bottom end. No result. I went back to the bathroom and opened the window. I saw a strange sight, even for this peculiar house, and I began to think the builder must have been more than eccentric. He must have been plain crazy.

The waste pipe ran down the wall for about one yard. Beneath it was another pipe with a sort of open cup at the top to catch the water as it jumped from the top pipe. This meant that both ends would be frozen, as well as the wide cup, already full of ice.

Yet we had to use the bath. I boiled a kettle of water and leaned out from the window. I was just about to hurl it over the pipe when I realized that I was exactly one yard from our neighbours' door, and if someone stepped outside they'd get it literally in the neck. I stationed Mervyn by the door with a red flag.

Kettle after kettle went down those wretched pipes. I thawed them at last, and this had to be done regularly as we had a hard winter. We sat in the draughty house, shivering and grumbling, all except Gypsy. This odd little animal loved the temperature to drop below zero, and the only time she wanted to go out was when we were knee-deep in snow.

It was natural that we should sometimes dream of a different way of living, a nicer house. It was Kay who started us on this tack, when she said one day that she hated to ask her friends home. I tried to tell her that it didn't matter, that nice people don't mind where you live, but how could a girl of her age understand that? Her school friends were the daughters of garage proprietors, tradesmen and the like, and if their god is money, well, they're not the only ones. I know this doesn't sound like *Little Women*, but life is unlike *Little Women*.

For her birthday I decided to give Kay a party; this time, I vowed, she'd have the best. So I really went to town. I made her a new dress, I bought food, mostly little sausages on sticks, as Kay said cakes and jellies were not now *à la mode* for girls' parties. We bought some pretty invitation cards and Kay took them to school. All the girls were pleased, she said.

The big day came. It was Saturday, and it had been snowing all night. Kay put on her new dress and I set out the food.

We waited in happy expectancy. Half past four, and there came a knock on the door. Kay ran to answer it. She came back with Jane, who lived next door and went to an ordinary council school, as we still called them in Hicktown.

We waited. Five o'clock. Kay looked a little apprehensive. "It's still snowing," I said, comfortingly. "They're bound to be late."

"Why?" asked Phil. "They all have big cars."

"They might get stuck in the snow," said Mervyn.

Six o'clock. Kay's head was high, but the light of expectancy was leaving her eyes. I said, brightly, "Shall we start on the sausages? I'm sure they've all been held up by the bad weather."

We moved to the table and ate, and afterwards Jane and Kay played snakes and ladders. No one else came.

Strange how odd moments stick in our minds. Perhaps they are important moments. When I think of Byfield Road now I see several pairs of eyes, Jane's questioning and knowing, Phil's suddenly sharp, Mervyn's bewildered.

But the saddest thing in the world are the eyes of a little girl who waits in vain for her friends to come to her party.

Some time before this I had been to see the headmistress of her school to tell her that I could no longer pay the fees. "Leave her here, she must not be taken away, we'll waive the fees," said that good lady. I was grateful, and wondered why Kay wasn't.

Only later, much, much later, did I learn that, when on each new day of term the headmistress gave out the bills, Kay was the only girl to sit and not receive a bill. And one day one of her delightful friends asked, "Are you a charity child?"

The boys didn't seem to have this trouble to quite the same extent; schoolboys seem to be less catty than girls, and their main interest is always who is to be in the football/cricket/ rugger team. But I remembered my own childhood and the great gulf that separated the respectable poor from those who had to be given free boots (publicly, in school). We all looked down on those freeboot children, though most of us were just one notch above the awful dividing line. I suppose the truth is that we needed free boots but pretended we didn't; the others, at rock bottom, could not pretend any longer. And this pretence makes all the difference.

I understood now why my mother had pinched and scraped (her own expression) to avoid charity, but it isn't easy to explain to people who ask why everyone doesn't take advantage of all those free offers. It's just that, when given a public charity, you somehow become the lowest form of life in everyone's eyes, even the rest of the poor. It is there in attitudes, and it is not imagined, that I promise you. So I never once let my children apply for free school dinners, not to stand in shame before their playmates. Keep up the pretence. Pretence hides a multitude of sins. Pretence that we're not poor. Pretence that we're not bitter or self-pitying. All the time reality swept under the carpet, and our consciences appeased by the thought that the poor are happy really, look how they laugh —and anyway they can't be as poor as all that if they won't apply for free dinners.

But we discovered that being brave and cheerful and happy

in the face of adversity is not enough. Not in England. One has
to Keep up Appearances. We dreamed of another home, in
another area.

When I saw the advert it seemed the answer to a prayer.
"Cottage rent free in return for a little housework." The
address was Cornell Place, a huge house, now with a new
owner and turned into flats.

I rushed down to see him. It was a long way from Byfield
Road, way out in the country, which would mean bus fares.
But it seemed a slice of heaven. Cornell Place was surrounded
by old trees, while further along were a squat little church
and a few cottages hiding shyly between the trees. There was
no clanging, no smell, no grime, just peace and beauty.

The owner took me inside the hall. He was, he told me,
very fond of the sea, and went sailing every summer, so for
several months we'd just be caretaking.

We chatted awhile. I told him of my circumstances and
mentioned Mervyn's poor health, which was one reason I'd
welcome a job where I could be at home. He was sympathetic,
and seemed interested in Mervyn. "He'll be able to come
with me on my yacht," he said. "I'm always in need of a
crew."

I gaped in astonishment, and thought what a lucky break
for Mervyn, sailing on a private yacht. I dreamed for a while,
and the owner enlarged on the work involved.

He occupied the whole of the ground floor, and he showed
me round huge rooms all containing lots of furniture to be
dusted and polished. There was his bedroom, and the bedrooms of the two friends who were staying with him on a
semi-permanent basis. There were long passages, a wide hall,
a yard outside, all to be cleaned every day. He would expect
me to do all his washing, and that of his friends—"You
could do it at your place" (using my washing machine and
electricity). He needed cooking done. "Good plain food.
Home-made cakes and so on."

I tried to reckon on how long it would take me to get
through all this. He told me benignly, "Should get through
it in the mornings, and you'll have the rest of the time free,
except for weekends when I have friends to stay. If you
wouldn't mind helping then . . ."

"Oh no," I said, easily.

"Of course, we wouldn't treat you as a—" he paused

delicately, not quite able to bring himself to say the word servant. I'm not sure why, for that is what I would be, doing the work which in former days would have been done by two housemaids, upper and under, parlour-maid, cook, laundry woman and odd-job man. I'm surprised he didn't ask me to dig the garden.

Yet I was tempted. He mentioned that hundreds of people had been ringing about the job; we were all willing to work like navvies to get ourselves a home. But it was beautiful, so different from Byfield Road. And it would be better for the children. I could be at home with Mervyn when he was ill, and Kay's friends would consider it quite in order to visit a tumble-down old cottage in the grounds of a mansion. I could remember the time when to live in a cottage was very low indeed; by now it was becoming trendy.

"The rest of the house is divided into flats," said the owner. "There are no dogs allowed." He was gazing at me earnestly. "What I really want is a *good* woman," he said, and I looked at him, startled. I had been interviewed by many bosses, of all shapes and sizes, but this was the first time one had referred to a good woman. If he meant a good worker, that was fair enough, and this was what he paid for. Anything else was my own affair, so I did not impress him with my goodness. I did not belong to my mother's knee-bending generation, when the morals of the lower orders were of great concern to those above, especially the ones who took them to bed as part of their duties. In the ensuing silence he asked me if I'd like to see the cottage.

The cottages had once been stables and looked it, a row of four, all joined together. An artist, said the owner, lived in one of them. I looked over the cottage which would be ours. It was big enough to accommodate one good-sized horse, nothing more. It had peeling wallpaper and damp ceilings. "I could decorate it," I said doubtfully, as though I hadn't had enough decorating to last me a lifetime.

But there was the wonderful view . . . He was looking at me. "As you were the first, I have given you the first refusal. Can you let me know as soon as possible?"

"I'll ask the children," I said.

Kay was desperately keen. She was ashamed of Byfield Road. She didn't understand why she was somehow an out-sider now, for Kay couldn't bear to be outside. Who can?

Hicktown was sharply divided into neat little sections. The nobs of Perronporth Road, whose children all passed for the town's grammar school, thus saving their parents the fees their own parents had had to pay at the same school; lower middles and working classes in the nicer suburbs, whose children went to fee-paying schools if they couldn't get into the grammar; and the rest, which meant Byfield Road and the council estates, nearly all of whose children went to secondary moderns. Kay fitted into none of these sections; her school friends didn't want to know her address, while her road-mates looked askance at her school uniform.

"Please let's go," said Kay. "Please!" The boys were keen too, though not for social reasons. Mervyn, being a poet, would wander through the world never even knowing there were such distinctions in housing, and Philly was still at junior school where even doctors' children went; junior schools were democratic—the division came with the senior moves, when the professionals' children had to make their way in the world via universities.

I thought our move might be agreeable. I could let the house. I'd be at home with Mervyn. I pushed away the prospect of all that work.

The next day a big car drew up outside and the owner stepped out and knocked at our door. I introduced Kay.

He nodded. "Have you made up your mind?" he asked.

"Yes. I think we'll come."

"Good." He turned and Gypsy walked in. Or, to be honest, rushed in, barking her stupid little head off. He asked, somewhat unnecessarily, "You have a dog?"

"Yes," I answered. "She's no trouble."

Gypsy barked to prove it, and the owner asked, "She?" And then, "Is it a—" pausing delicately—"a lady dog?"

"Yes," I said, wanting to laugh.

"I'm sorry, but I don't allow any dogs. And a—a lady—"

"But I thought that was in the flats. There is a strong gate at the cottage—" I had noticed that, and thought it would be ideal for Gypsy.

"That's my rule," he said, firmly. "No dogs. Think it over. Ring me tomorrow." And he went on his way.

We talked it over that evening as we sat round the smoking fire. We didn't want to part with Gypsy; she was beginning to be a necessary part of our life. Sharing our hardships, one of the family. She was odd but she was ours. Happiness was a funny little scottie who would defend us to the death if she ever worked out in her small muddled head where death was coming from. She stared at us now, solemnly, but she didn't lick our hands or beg. It wasn't her way.

"We can't let her go," said Phil.

"Go?" asked Kay. "To be destroyed?" She looked ready to cry.

I went to bed undecided. Wouldn't it be better for the children? I thought of Mervyn, sailing on the yacht, having good sea-air, being helped by the owner . . .

But I knew we couldn't let Gypsy go. We couldn't afford to.

The next day I rang Cornell Place. "I'm sorry," I said wretchedly, as my dreams of gracious living—*"Yes, my son goes sailing, private yacht, you know"*—vanished for the sake of my dog Gypsy.

"I am too," said the owner, "but those are the rules."

Sighing, I went back to the old house, the frozen pipes, the dark rooms, the second-class citizenship.

5

BUREAUCRACY

But man, proud man,
Drest in a little brief authority,
Most ignorant of what he's most assured,
His glossy essence, like an angry ape,
Plays such fantastic tricks before high heaven,
As makes the angels weep.

—SHAKESPEARE

MERVYN HAD BEEN a brilliant child. At four years
he had taught himself to tell the time and to read. At school
he was always top of the class, and his teachers thought him
a wonder. His poems won first prizes in Hicktown's Festival
of Arts, one adjudicator, a well-known B.B.C. figure, writing,
*"A magnificent and baffling achievement for one so young
...a child who is a true poet... This boy should be
ENCOURAGED. Promise such as he shows is rare indeed ...
it would be a very great shame if, through lack of help and
encouragement, this boy should allow his view of the world
to become dulled or withered, or driven inward. If this were to
happen, many of us might well be the poorer."*
I watched all this with disquiet. Possessing no medical
knowledge, I thought that Mervyn seemed to have too big
a brain in too small a body. It burned feverishly through his
dark eyes. I compared him to a small car with an extremely
high-powered engine, and I thought, "If the engine is allowed
to run full out it will break the car, but if we hold back the
engine that itself will be damaged. What is the answer when
the brain and body don't match?"
The answer was epilepsy.
Handicaps vary, and so does the reaction to them. A blind
person meets with sympathy and kindness, and a cripple is
genuinely pitied. We don't poke fun at mentally ill patients
these days. But an epileptic is somehow regarded as a leper,
an untouchable in the caste system of illnesses, even though

one person in two hundred will suffer some form of epilepsy in his lifetime. We were unlucky that we picked an illness no one knew much about, and the majority cared less.

I once read a holiday brochure. "People subject to fits not admitted," it stated. Most convalescent homes refuse to take epileptics, as do practically all landladies, and employers. I even read of a child refused admission to Sunday School. I used to wonder if there would be a notice on the gates of heaven: "People subject to fits not admitted."

Mervyn passed the 11-plus and went to grammar school. But by this time he was heavily drugged and soon began to fall behind with his work. This worried him tremendously, and he *tried*. Oh God, how he tried.

We went to Hicktown's hospital, which had been built just before the second world war to accommodate the huge numbers of forces casualties anticipated. It stood empty for most of the time, except for air-raid victims. Now, switched to civilian use, it was always full. We waited in a cheerless prefabricated waiting-room to see the pediatrician.

He was what my old-fashioned mother would have called a gentleman. Not that that made much difference to his qualifications, but I must say that in Hicktown doctors' manners to the plebs often left much to be desired. The pediatrician was kind to Mervyn, and when I asked for the truth gave it to me, leaving me gasping. He wanted him to go to the city hospital for an electro-encephalogram.

We went. In an old, grim building we were led down some stone steps to a room with barred windows. I wondered if we had made a mistake and were entering the county jail. Mervyn was told to lie on a bed, and a strange contraption like an old-fashioned permanent-waving machine was placed on his head, but this one dealt with brain waves. Lights were flashed in his eyes, and it was all faintly reminiscent of mediaeval torture. We reported back to the pediatrician and he told me Mervyn was epileptic. I asked him what was the cause. He said, drily, "If we knew that we'd know how to cure it."

So Mervyn was drugged, but he still had fits. They usually occurred in the morning, when I would send Philly to my parents' house, and my father would come up while I went to work. Sometimes Mervyn had a fit at school, and would be sent home in an ambulance. Other times he'd be sent straight to hospital, and a policeman would come to tell me. To this day the sight of a blue uniform coming to the door fills me with terror.

One sunny day, when Mervyn was fifteen, and hoping to pass a few O-levels at least, he had a fit in school and was sent home. The next day I received a letter from his headmaster saying would I please not send him back, as the fits upset the children. By the same post was a card from a school-pal. "Dear Merv, Sorry you are ill, hope to see you Monday."

I hardly knew how to break the news to Mervyn; he believed so fervently in all the school taught about honour. It was a harsh way to learn what sceptical Philly had known since birth, and I don't think he ever recovered from the blow.

So he was at home. I had to give up my job. And I came up against bureaucracy.

Out of the blue I received a letter informing me that all my family allowances were to be stopped. I was further informed by the Ministry that as I was living apart from my husband he could claim them if he so wished. In other words, when a mother was living with her husband and didn't need the allowances quite so much she, and she alone, was able to claim them. When she was on her own and desperate for money, then the husband could claim too. Said the Ministry, "As you are separated from your husband the children are eligible to be included in his family as well as yours, although they are living with you."

This was the first of many letters which were to arrive out of the blue to inform me that because of Section 3, Part 2X, reference YZ, what I had fondly imagined to be a settled income, however low, was to be adjusted (downwards) or stopped.

I started a lengthy business of writing to Ministries, departments A to Z, wondering meanwhile how those people manage who aren't very literate. I suppose they just lose out.

After three months I was duly told, "Your husband has been approached and has agreed that the children be included in your family . . . If at any time in the future your husband notifies this department that he is no longer agreeable, then the Ministry will decide in whose family the children are to be included." This is what I call living on a precipice.

The doctors had been fighting for Mervyn meanwhile, and

finally he was sent for a short time to a special school for, oddly, the blind. (Schools for epileptics are not in great supply.) I was presented with a bill for £20 for his clothing. I informed the education authority that I could not pay and was told to apply to National Assistance. The Assistance people said they could give money only for essential clothing, and two vests were deemed sufficient by this body; the school demanded four. I reported back to education. "Can you ask the WVS?" they asked. I said no, but if they'd give me a letter of refusal I'd take the matter to court, for my husband to pay. Oddly, I didn't hear any more—the education people paid.

Mervyn finished his school and was sent to a nearby rehabilitation unit, when one family allowance was stopped. again, I asked why. I was told :

"Attendance at this Unit does not appear to satisfy the requirements of the Family Allowances Acts in so far as 'Full Time Training' is concerned. If, however, he should commence 'Full Time Training' as an *Apprentice*, and you consider him eligible for inclusion, you should notify this Department immediately. Meanwhile he has been excluded from Family Allowances purposes with effect from Tuesday 17th July 1962.

"Yours faithfully,

"Ministry of Pensions & National Insurance."

The rehabilitation unit recommended that Mervyn should go back to school. The County Council refused to send him. The Ministry of Labour would not allow him to take a course of training because he was handicapped. (His consultant said he should use his brain as much as possible.) The Disablement Officer told him to pay for a course out of his own pocket.

So he was forced to stay at home, untrained, unemployed, with a high I.Q., walking his weary way to the labour exchange to draw £2 10s. od. a week National Assistance, which had to be paid at the labour exchange as he had to register for work. If he'd had stamps on his card he could have drawn £3 7s. od. dole, as it is always called in Hicktown. But he would never get stamps on his card if he couldn't get employment . . .

Insurance stamps. Surely there are no lovelier words in the English language. I used to say them over and over. When I started *working*, as against being a housewife, I said, "Now I must not be ill for a year, until I have enough insurance stamps to give me payment . . ." Then I found it didn't work that way; stamps were never counted from the first week you bought them, somehow you always paid lots and lots for nothing till they started counting . . .

So with Mervyn ill, and at home, I had no alternative but to stay at home too, and for this there is no insurance. His illness was such that he could not be left alone, for he might fall in the fire, or downstairs, or drown in the bath.

I read through a National Assistance handbook. It said, "It has been the aim of the National Assistance Board to ensure, as far as possible, that no one eligible for their help lives below the level set by Parliament in the Regulations. The peculiar problem in seeking to achieve this aim has been the reluctance of some people to approach the Board . . . The Board emphasises that no one need lose their self-respect by applying . . ."

So, faced with the alternative prospect of starving, I decided to apply for National Assistance. Yet I did feel I was losing my self-respect, and none of the Board's officers at any time said or did anything that might make me change that view.

The working-class is divided into two main groups, the Respectable and the Low-Class (their own definition). The Low-Class is the one you usually hear about, although it is the smallest, and consists of the inadequate, the misfits, the not-too-bright, the criminals and the few scroungers who are always willing to tell the tale in return for what they can pick up. These are all scorned out of hand by the Respectable, whose own hard times come simply from lack of work or lack of breadwinners, but their scorn holds a touch of fear, for they are only a step away and they know it. We all hate the class we may at any time fall into, and it is ironic that most of the National Assistance Board officials are drawn from the lower middle class, as are most of the other local officials— civil servants, shop-owners, teachers, etc. "Our greatest dictators are those who have just jumped away from us," say the Respectable workers, sardonically.

The Respectable workers refuse to have any truck with probation officers, welfare officers (unless to do with health), Social Security, and anything which brings an official in a car to the door. If visited by such officials you lose face, as these deal with criminals and delinquents. The neighbours look down their noses and mentally push you down with the Low-Class.

So your Respectable workers hang on to their pride and dignity like grim death, grumbling the while about those who, in their eyes, get on better.

"She's been down telling the tale again, got a new set of furniture." "Ah, them sort can get owt." There is no sympathy from those who would die rather than beg, who want nothing but to be left alone to live their own lives in a responsible way, which they are quite capable of doing provided they have the money for this purpose. Yet they all know that, however much pride and dignity is held to be a highly desirable form of English life, in trouble you always get on better if you *cringe*. Tell a sob story to your friends and they will love you the more for it. You can be forgiven for doing wrong if you are suitably repentant, and this does not seem to me to be a part of religion as much as a part of human nature. You cannot forgive a person who both breaks the rules and doesn't care.

This is something your natural scrounger knows instinctively. He knows there is something in human nature which encourages him to grovel. That is why he resists authority's attempts to get him to be proud and dignified again, and it is why those who deal with the unfortunates of life should watch themselves just as carefully as those to whom they minister.

The Respectable worker's attitude, coupled with all the pride and dignity, is not altogether due to the old Poor Law/ workhouse fear. It is more realistic. Once you are down, right down with Edna the Inebriate Woman, it is pretty nearly impossible to rise again. If you become known as a bad risk you can never expect to buy anything else on H.P.; you will find it difficult to get a house, even a job, and it is rumoured even to affect your children when entering for the 11-plus or for anything that will get them on and out, when the teacher's hand is poised carefully over the section marked "home background". Once down there you have, in short, lost your security for ever.

The poor may have ungenerous attitudes; they fight each other, each little group grasping for its own piece of the cake and devil take the hindmost. It's a matter of survival.

So all in all I wasn't very happy about losing my self-respect. It made me prickly and aggressive from the word go.

The local office was situated in a main road, and as I went in and joined the queue people chattered and said to go to the man, the woman would give you nowt. My draw gave me the woman.

I stepped into a little office and was told to sit down. "You've given up your job?" she asked.

"Yes, my son is ill."

"Doesn't your husband pay maintenance to you?"

"Only to the children."

"Have you an order for maintenance?"

"No. I'm going to divorce him."

"You should apply for an order. Apply now. You can't expect the Board to pay when your husband should." The woman wrote busily. "Someone will call to see you. Next, please."

He was a little man who called, quite friendly, a bit self-important. He asked if he might see my bankbook. "You're joking, of course," I said, politely.

"Your rates paper, electricity bills, details of family allowances, husband's payments, rent book—"

"I'm buying the house," I said.

"We can't help you to buy a house, you know. We can pay towards the interest, that's all."

"I see. But if we were paying £20 a week rent you could pay all that?"

"Humph," said the little man, testily. I always ask too many questions.

"How do I pay the mortgage, then?"

"You must ask the building society to wait."

"Wait until when?"

"Until you can repay them."

"But if I get into debt . . . if I get in arrears I'll be turned out." *What happens then, Assistance Board? Homes for the children, taken into care?* I was silent. Don't look a gift horse too deep in the mouth. For however much the National Assistance Board's booklets might talk grandly about its being our right, the Board's officers never seemed to see it that way. To them it was a gift, doled out by a generous government to thankless paupers. "We paupers keep you in work," I used to say, light-heartedly. "Who pays your wages but the tax-paying public?"—a way of looking at things which hadn't occurred to them. *Handy-dandy, which is the thief?*

I asked the little man how much I should get. "Oh, I can't tell you *that*," he said, mysteriously, and a little horrified. He departed, and I duly received through the post an order book giving me £3 1s. 6d. to be cashed at the nearby post office, to be drawn before the eager stares of the neighbours.

The weather had been dry for quite a time. Now it began to rain and the water seeped through the kitchen roof, dripping mournfully on the floor. The tank overflowed regularly, and soon we kept all our buckets and bowls beneath it. The chimney smoked, and the rising winds blew down the old fence.

The National Assistance man visited me regularly to enquire about my circumstances. Wondering why, I found in my Handbook: *"Each allowance has to be calculated by reference to the individual's circumstances, and the basic amount adjusted where necessary by means of discretionary additions to meet special needs. The Board have a statutory duty to promote the welfare of people receiving assistance, their officers have to be able to identify needs requiring reference to other agencies and other special action. For these reasons the Board have discharged their functions primarily through home visiting."* I thought he was coming because he suspected I might be swindling the Board.

I went to my lawyer and told him the Assistance people said I should claim maintenance for myself from husband through a magistrate's court, and we had a little conversation about such payments.

"The court will take the man's wages and circumstances and the needs of mother and children into account," said he, "and will award maintenance to a maximum of £7 10s. 0d. for the mother and £2 10s. 0d. for each child. In practice these maximums are rarely awarded because the court knows that if the amount is set too high the father will not pay, and magistrates know from experience how difficult it is to extract any payments from a husband who just disappears."

"But can't it be stopped from his wages?" I asked.

"Not when the order is first granted. If the husband disappears before the hearing there may be great difficulty in serving the summons."

"I do see that," I said, drily.

"If at any time maintenance is four weeks in arrears, the wife can ask for an attachment of earnings order. Another summons is served on the husband. The court will then consider the man's own financial needs, the needs of 'those for whom he must or reasonably may provide—' "

"Such as a second wife, ten children, an old mother, not to mention twelve relatives in dire straits," I put in.

"And will then specify a 'protected earnings rate' below which his earnings may not be reduced. Courts tend to set a high protected earnings rate."

"Who goes hungry, then?" I asked. "Don't tell me, let me guess."

"The maintenance can only be paid out of the margin of income received by the man in any week above the 'protected earnings'. The wife loses her entitlement to maintenance if the husband does not earn more than the protected earnings rate in any week. Furthermore, the husband is entitled to have his earnings made up to the protected earnings rate for any week in which his earnings are below this rate, from the margin of his income above this rate in the following weeks, before he is liable to pay maintenance to his wife."

"Funny, isn't it?" I asked. "Funny peculiar, I mean. What about this business of a man claiming money when his wife goes off with another man?"

"You mean damages from the High Court?"

"Damages, that's right. Why can't I claim damages?"

"There's nothing in law," began my poor lawyer, looking over his spectacles.

"If I went off with another man and the judge awarded my husband £2,000 damages," I said, "why am I worth nothing *now*? If I'm worth that much to him, why shouldn't he pay it to me if he loses the case? Do you follow?"

"No," said my lawyer.

"Well, let's just apply for maintenance for the old floor-scrubber," I said.

"As your divorce is pending, it will have to be alimony, and we claim from the registrar," said my lawyer.

I didn't know who the registrar was, but he didn't place much value on me. I was awarded £2 a week wergild from my husband, which was immediately stopped from my

Assistance payment, leaving me £1 1s. 6d. And my husband at once dropped his undefended suit and applied to defend. (He had said he was determined not to pay me *anything*, and no judge would make him.) His application was granted, and we were back to square one in the divorce proceedings, having to start all over again.

Baffled and amazed at women's rights, lack of, I sat down and wrote an angry letter to a Sunday quality newspaper. This was published, and for the next few weeks I wondered what had hit me. Letters poured in from women, happily married women, storming about the lack of help in high places. "We want justice," cried one, "not charity." "Welfare State!" raged another. "Whose welfare, that of paid officials?" Men wrote too, including one who wanted me to "start something". But, dear Lord, I didn't have time. Some offered advice, some help and holidays. Some wrote to their M.P.s. And I ruined all their lovely letters with tears, for they made me feel like a human being again.

The M.P.s wrote back to their constituents and said in the main that they thought this mother could obtain increased help from National Assistance. (How? By storming the Bastille?) There were also voluntary organisations able to help, if their attention were drawn to unfortunate cases. And it would seem that the court might well order an additional amount to be paid by the father towards the children's keep.

I had never thought of applying for charity, but as the writers had been so kind in pointing out where I could apply, and also that some benevolent funds were very wealthy, I thought I could hardly moan about being hard up if I refused to take help available. I wrote to several places, including two who had written to me first.

First of all was Dr Barnardo's. This association had written to me after my letter was published, asking if I would like to apply for their outside help of up to 15s. a week. I replied that I would and was visited by one of their welfare officers. Then I was sent a question sheet to fill in. I did this, and they lost it. They wrote again and so did I, and another form was sent, together with the remark that it was most important that we should give our religious denomination.

I filled in the second form and carefully stated our religion. This was to the effect that, although the children had been baptised R.C. because their father had been a Catholic (non-practising), neither they nor I were practising Catholics, nor did we wish to be. Back came the reply three months after my first application.

"I must explain that we have a long-standing engagement with the Roman Catholic authorities to refer Catholic cases to them, they in turn passing on to us any Protestant applications which they may receive. I am afraid that it is not possible for us to depart from our ruling in such matters, and this means that I can only offer to refer your case to the Roman Catholic Authorities in London, namely the Crusade of Rescue."

But we were not Catholics, as I said, nor did we want to be, and I hardly saw the point of applying to a faith to which we did not belong. So while the faiths were bargaining about our souls, our bodies were left as they were. Perhaps I should have tried the Salvation Army—I don't think they demand that one should wear their uniform before succour is given.

I had a letter from the British Legion asking if I required help. To my yes please, they sent someone to see me, then wrote the following letter: "Having received the report of our investigator who recently called upon you following publication of your letter, it is with very sincere regret that we have to inform you that the British Legion cannot be of any assistance to you because neither you nor your husband has any service qualifications which can bring your case within the scope of the terms of the British Legion Royal Charter. We are sorry . . ."

My husband had served in the Air Force for four years.

I received a letter from a lady sending a booklet about an organisation which helped "many hundreds of deprived children to become happy citizens of Canada and Australia . . ." and wanted to "give the Commonwealth good British migrants". I knew the suggestion was made sincerely, but wondered why I should have to send my children to another country in order to give them a chance to grow up in decent conditions.

One lady suggested that we should apply to whichever force my husband served in during the war. So I applied to the Royal Air Force Benevolent Fund. I was informed that they could not help as immediately after the war ended he had returned to the country from which he had volunteered for service.

I applied to a local working-class charity, run by a pub, a man visited me, and without more ado I was given vouchers for food.

I had previously applied to a benevolent fund into which my husband paid, and after months of correspondence, when many letters were lost, I did finally get a payment towards Kay's school fees. Then they advised me to write to the R.A.F.

Finally it was whittled down to whether Kay could receive help towards her school fees. A letter from the Ministry of Education, External Relations and General Branch, read, "Your application of the 10th May has been carefully and sympathetically considered. We have consulted the Ministry of Pensions and N.I., and enquired whether anything could be done under the Pensions Scheme. It appears, however, that only disabled ex-servicemen in receipt of continuing weekly payments are eligible for educational grants. In the circumstances I very much regret . . ."

(If I *had* received any financial help from any of these benevolent funds, I was told it would have immediately been stopped from the National Assistance payments, so we'd have been back at square one.)

At this time Kay had sat for her 11-plus for admittance to grammar school, and had been turned down. A friend told me that she had seen her name on the passed list, but when I rang the headmaster he said she had been a borderline case, and couldn't she stay at her private school?

The reason I would have preferred her either to stay on at her present school or pass for grammar school was that she was feeling just a little deprived at that time. On the whole I thought, with the headmistress, that she'd be better to stay where she was, that it would upset her more to leave and be cast out, so to speak. So I made one last try about her education. I asked the local education authorities, who are empowered to pay fees, if they would consider paying Kay's. The fees were not high, incidentally. They replied :

"Your letter was duly discussed by the Education Committee at its last meeting. The following resolution was passed :

"ASSISTANCE TO PUPILS. Submitted an application for assistance in the payment of fees under Section 81.
"RECOMMENDED. That no assistance be granted towards the cost of education of a type for which the pupil has not qualified, having had due opportunity to do so, within the Authority's arrangements for allocation to secondary education.
"Yours faithfully, Education Officer."

So Kay left the private school, and went to a secondary modern. She did no more ballet.

My letter to the Sunday paper produced one reply signed "Ex-social worker", stern in the tradition of lady members of the race. She wrote:

"The letter leaves me thinking this mother could do more for herself, and I think the following points are relevant:

"It should not be much hardship for a young child to wear second-hand clothing if the mother is good with her needle." (But what if the mother is not?) "When this mother's children approach their teens, however, I suggest that she encourages them to take a paper round.

"This mother no doubt feels her life is difficult and dreary, but is she, I wonder, remembering to make maximum use of local facilities, such as parks, museums and libraries?

"Poverty is relative, and there is a large section of the working, tax-paying community whose living standards are not high. Many men in various trades receive, after a full week's work, little more than this mother's income (a glance at the Ministry of Labour's booklet on Wages confirms this)."

I love you too, Patience Strong.

I would like to say that I spent many a happy hour glancing at that Ministry of Labour booklet, being joyful and contented because other people were also hard up. But the thought of poverty being relative (relative to what?) doesn't help *at all*. It didn't help to make my ends meet. I was to notice that many of the Assistance people I met were to offer this same dubious consolation. Coming to the logical conclusion, I wrote to the chairman of the Assistance Board, no less, and asked if he used this argument with his wife when she wanted something new. For if he had written and said that he lived on less than £10 a week, but was quite content because he knew there were so many others in want, then I

would have taken a real hard look at this line of reasoning.
It takes a Christian to preach the Christian faith.

A woman M.P. also wrote to the Chairman of the Board,
and he wrote to me, and after some lively correspondence I
did learn just what I was getting and why, which up to now
had been shrouded in secrecy. My total income from all
sources could not be more than £8 7s. 6d. a week, so from
this my husband's payments and my family allowances were
deducted. My needs were assessed under the regulations of the
scale rates of £2 13s. 6d. for myself, a total of £3 16s. od.
for the children (as my husband paid £4 8s. od. he was in
fact subsidising the Board) and £1 18s. od. for outgoings on
the house. The standard Assistance rates were intended to
allow for all ordinary maintenance expenses such as coal and
electricity, and making good ordinary wear and tear of clothing. The chairman agreed with me that there were things for
which the Board's grants did not provide. The regulations
allow for repayments of mortgage interest but not capital,
on the grounds that buying by instalments is a form of saving,
and as such not a matter for the State to subsidise. (Why
hadn't I a subsidised council house?) It was well worth remembering that not all men in full-time work who are bringing up families can afford commitments of this sort. (Women's
Lib., please note.)

This subtle insinuation that not only are there Others Worse
Off Than You but that somehow you are doing wrong in
trying to improve your lot must, I think, be taught at the
school for training National Assistance officials. They all
bring it in sooner or later. "My wife can't afford new clothes,
ha ha." "I can't afford a new suit." So, I am sure, did the
Poor Law Guardians speak to the trembling paupers. Do
You Think You're the Only Person Who Can't Afford a
Good Dinner? How Dare you be in Want anyway? And,
Once In, How Dare You Try to Get Out by Helping Yourself? You should not Buy Anything, and certainly not a
House. If you haven't anywhere to live you can go to the
Workhouse Institution and put your children in care, which
will cost the country twenty times as much as if you were
allowed to buy a house. We'll Show You.

However, this hobnobbing with M.P.s did have some effect.
The local manager of the Board came to see me, and he was
a nice man who made no mention of poverty being relative.

My house was inspected and I was given a payment of £15 for "improvements", which meant that I could have the faulty electric switches repaired—they were actually dangerous, especially as water dripped on to them through the ceiling. I was able to get the rain-tank pipes cut off, so we weren't quite so damp downstairs, although the bedrooms were still damp. I was given £3 to buy a second-hand chest of drawers, this being deemed to be all the additional furniture I needed, and for this I was duly grateful. But let us remember, for all the rule-book talk of officers visiting us to see what discretionary grants they can give, these grants would not have been given had I not written to a newspaper.

Finally, Mervyn was sent away to a school for epileptics. A doctor had been trying to get him there for some time, but had been held back by arguments between the Ministry of Labour and the County Council about who was to pay.

Now, being without work myself, I was asked if I would like to take a refresher shorthand/typing course for six months. I jumped at this eagerly. I should be *paid* for doing it, £6 5s. od. for self and two children. If I'd been a man I'd have had £7. But this was higher than Assistance, as maintenance payments and family allowances did not have to be deducted.

Unfortunately, my shorthand was so rusty that I found I needed to start right at the beginning. The class I went to held a two-year course. I had only six months, and the methods of teaching were so different now, it was like learning something altogether new.

I worked hard and practised at home, and at six months I had gone right through the course and had a speed of 80. I called in at the labour exchange to enquire about jobs, only to be told that 80 was a junior speed; at my age I would not get a job unless I had a speed of *at least* 100. I asked, therefore, if I could have a three-weeks' extension to enable me to reach the required speed. I received the following reply: "Referring to your enquiry, I have to inform you that the Department are unable to agree to an extension of your training course as you have already reached the V.T.S. standard of 80 w.p.m., and 35 in typing. Yours faithfully, Labour Exchange."

So the course and the money were wasted, for no employer would take on a woman of my age without a speed of 120 w.p.m.—with too many people chasing too few jobs, they didn't need to.

Now I was applying for work again. I told everyone I was a shorthand typist, and when asked if I had a speed of 100/120 I lied unblushingly and said yes. Then I was given a test and proved wrong.

Round and round the offices I went, on a mad roundabout of taking tests, failing, getting more nervous, feeling I'd fail and failing all the more, begging for a job, willing to do anything . . .

One day I went to the city. And that day I didn't care. There must be a law which gives you what you want when you don't bother about it any longer, refusing it when you're desperate, some unkind sadistic twirl of Providence. So I got a job.

I went to an agency. I didn't know much about agencies, those offices which find you a job if you pay your first week's salary. There were none in Hicktown. Now I wouldn't go anywhere else. The girl told me of a firm which wanted copy typists at £9 a week. That was a lot of money for the provinces.

I arrived at the firm, a huge place with a personnel department as large as some factories. We all sat on comfortable chairs and read magazines.

I was given a huge form to fill in, writing all my life story. This put me in a bad temper to start with. I had knocked two years off my age, and I found myself unable to reckon up the correct answer to "Date you started your first school."

I handed it back to the girl and said, "I can't remember that far back."

"Don't worry," she said, easily. "I'll fill it in." She wrote busily and I looked over her shoulder. In the spot marked "Observations' 'she wrote "Rather sour." She was right, too. I was sour as little green apples that day.

"Will you come and see Miss Matchit?" she asked pleasantly, and wonderingly I passed all the other candidates still struggling with their forms and followed her to Miss Matchit, head of the typing pool.

I told this lady I wanted a job as a copy typist. She asked about shorthand. "Oh yes," I lied. "I can do 120."

She said, "Mr Baxet wants a secretary, he'll give you a little test. But he's not in. Can you come back this afternoon?"

My courage failed me. "No," I said. "I'll go if you haven't
anything for a copy typist."

"Oh, you need something better than that," she said, and
I grew ten feet tall, while I looked over my shoulder to see
if she was talking to anyone else.

She fetched a man. "We need a supervisor for the office," he
said. "Do you think you could do the job?"

"Of course," I said easily, knowing nothing about super-
vising.

"We'll give you a little typing test. Now, here's a type-
writer. If you'd like to practise on it for a moment to get used
to it."

They stood outside the glass cubicle, talking to each other.
At last Mr Bacon came in to where I had typed
nowishtimegrrghfkdjsl, and looked at it. "Shall we go over to
my office and discuss the salary?" he asked.

"But I haven't done the test," I said, startled.

"Oh, that's all right, I know a typist when I hear one."
And with nonchalant laughter we went to his office.

He mentioned children but I dismissed this airily, as though
I earned enough to pay for hired help. He knew very well
that I wouldn't earn enough to pay for help, but he let it
slide. He was desperate for a supervisor. I think I only got jobs
when employers were desperate.

We discussed terms, and I staggered out of the building
with the alarming news that I was to start working the following week at a salary of £12 a week.

We celebrated that night. We laughed and hurrahed and
bought sweets and chocolate and I wrote off to enquire about
a holiday.

"You see," I explained to my friend Mary, "when you've
been on your uppers for so long it's so marvellous to have
money again that you just have to spend it."

"I know," she said, gloomily. "That's why people write
to newspapers, bemoaning about paying the poor too much,
for they spend it on bingo."

"Until I was poor," I said grandly, "I never knew the
great desire, when a little money comes, to blue it all in. They
don't understand, either. Lead me to the bingo, Mary."

6

THE DIVORCE

So it comes that man, the coward, when he gathers to confer
With his fellow braves in council, dare not leave a place for her
Where, at war with Life and Conscience, he uplifts his erring
   hands
To some God of Abstract Justice—which no woman understands.
                                                      —KIPLING

A LOT OF people say there is one law for the rich and one
for the poor. I don't believe that. There is just one law, but
you get on better if you have plenty of money. Rich people
are granted divorces in weeks: I waited three years before
we reached court. The one thing that made it possible at all
was the fact that I had no difficulty in getting legal aid.

Three years is a long time, and I began to be restive long
before the end of it. So I took "Social Worker's" advice and
made full use of the library to delve more deeply into marriage
and divorce and the law. I also enrolled at a local university
(evenings) and came up with some interesting oddments.

English law has a continuous history which can be traced
back to Ethelbert, King of Kent, in the year 560, and sometimes it shows. True, some of the older methods of trial have
disappeared, such as ordeal by fire, when the accused had to
carry a red-hot iron a distance of nine feet and if the subsequent wound healed he was innocent, if not guilty. Like-
wise the ordeal by water, where he was bound and lowered
into a pool. If he sank a certain distance he was innocent, if
not guilty, and this survived until the seventeenth century as
a trial for witches. These happy rituals were conducted with
solemnity under the aegis of the Church.

In the Middle Ages the ecclesiastical courts were quite outside the control of the king. They dealt with the disciplining
of the clergy and with matrimonial causes. Following that
old warrior, Paul, the early Fathers seemed to have a
particular down on women, very different from their Master,

who not only made friends with the woman taken in adultery but challenged anyone without sin to cast the first stone. The Church turned its back on this bit of compassion, and sex became a thing of guilt and sin.

That this preoccupation with guilty sex has had a detrimental effect on women's lives cannot be denied. Writes Alex Comfort in *Sex and Society**, "Whatever Christianity may have contributed to the growth of our culture in other fields, it seems undeniable that in sexual morals and practice its influence has been less healthy than that of other world religions ... In English society it is only the most educated levels, and these only recently and superficially, which have ceased to regard all sexual activity as a source of guilt, sin, and dangerously deep-seated emotions, and its expressions as basically dangerous and hostile acts. The unconscious attitudes of the public hark back to the manifest psychopathy of the Alexandrian monks, to the dictum of St Anselm that woman is the torch of Satan, and to the concentration of all moral energies in resistance to the seduction of the flesh. The current sense of the word 'immoral' is an index of the underlying attitude of this culture.

"Another trait that exists prominently in Christian history is the emphasis on the value of suffering and self-abasement. The history of its doctrines and the circumstances of its foundation focused attention on pain and privation as means of atonement, but the deliberate seeking out of pain as a substitute for the claims of the flesh had no part in the earliest Apostolic teaching and seems to have originated in the asocial society of Roman North Africa rather than in the Jerusalem of Christ."

Nevertheless, in the robust Middle Ages, in England at least, the Church didn't have it all its own way, and women grew sadly independent. Most writers about law and women skip this interesting bit of information, but Paul Murray Kendall writes in *The Yorkist Age*† :

"If the manuals of manners insist that a wife must find her destiny within the character of Patient Griselda, the life of the age itself reveals that women, even as they were bringing child after child into the world, were often the study partners of their husbands' enterprises. In the towns, wives played

* Duckworth & Co. (1963).
† Allen & Unwin (1962).

an active part in business . . . Among the lower orders, wives often added to the family income by becoming brewers, bakers and tavern-keepers, and it is sad to relate that they were every bit as celebrated for their short weights and false quarts as their masculine rivals . . . Towns generally recognised the independence of married women in business. At Worcester and elsewhere husbands were exempted from financial liability in case their wives were sued as a consequence of their dealings. The wife was 'sole merchant'. When a married man was to be made a citizen of York, he appeared with his wife and both of them were admitted as 'free burgesses'. As in all ages, some husbands found their spouses only too masterful . . ."

Our legal system of marriage was born in the Middle Ages, while it was not until Lord Hardwick's Act in 1735 that a religious ceremony was made the condition of the legality of marriage in England. Briffault, in *The Mothers*,* says that in the early Christian church any suggestion that marriage should be regarded as a sacrament would have been blasphemy, and for many centuries the consent of both parties was sufficient to constitute a marriage.

By Victoria's time women's rights had sunk so low that when a husband promised "with all my worldly goods I thee endow" he was immediately given the right to take over all his wife's goods. He owned her, her property, her savings, her jewels and her income, and could legally support a mistress on his wife's earnings.

Sir Erskine Perry, the first man to bring a Married Woman's Property Bill before Parliament, in 1857, said: "Under the old English law there could be no doubt that a woman succeeded on equal terms, with women of other nations, to the property of her husband; she was entitled to a third of the land, and a third of the personal property. The decrees of legal tribunals, however, had abrogated this old law, and, by imperceptible degrees, had deprived married women of their rights, while allowing husbands to deal with wives' property as they thought fit. The law had not been changed by Act of Parliament, only by the decisions of the judges."

In 1857 a new civil court came into being, known as the Divorce Court, which took over the power of the ecclesiastical

* Allen & Unwin (1959).

court, but this by no means placed men and women in an equal position. Under it a husband could obtain a divorce on the ground of his wife's adultery alone, but the wife could only divorce her husband if he was proved to be guilty of adultery coupled with cruelty, bigamy, incest, desertion, rape, sodomy, or bestiality, and this remained in force until 1923, when a wife could divorce for adultery alone. The husband still had the right to treat his wife with the utmost cruelty, but unless he committed adultery she had no redress.

In a patriarchal society it is, perhaps, inevitable that women shall have little value and that adultery is held to be the only sin. When women dragged wagons of coal, underground in coal mines, by means of chains passed through their legs, it is said that the fact that they were in moral danger rather than the cruelty of the work influenced the powers of that period to put a stop to it. Whether women objected more to being raped or to being literally worked to death is not known. So perhaps it is not surprising that cruelty was not counted as sufficient grounds for divorce until 1937.

Sir Alan (then Mr A. P.) Herbert, when introducing the Matrimonial Causes Act, had said in 1935, "These laws of ours cannot be defended by reference to divine sanction, nor on the grounds of human needs, and they are based in the main on historical accidents, on antique prejudices, and upon the strange and almost bestial notion that the one thing which matters in married life is the sexual act and the only breach of the marriage obligation is the breach of the sexual relationship." This thinking is still the basis of much marriage advice, whether the problem is cruelty or adultery; the wife is asked if her husband's sexual needs are gratified, thus putting the blame for whatever goes wrong neatly on to her.

"One of the reasons given for the failure of community to take root in England lay in the fact that in origin it was based on the customs of those low in the social and economic scale. On the continent, these customs slowly made their way among the nobles. In England, the opposite was true. As Pollock and Maitland put it: 'In England, the law for the great becomes the law for all.' This dominating feudal and aristocratic principle has remained with us ever since, to trammel the law relating to matrimonial property and financial provision."*

* *The Inside of Divorce* by Bill Mortlock.

3—NHISG * *

The lower classes of England, while keeping their community life, have always been closer in attitudes to the aristocracy than to the middle-classes. The husband is head of the house, the wife is his property. Cruelty to the wife by the husband is not considered important either by the law or by the husband, and in the 1971 Divorce Reform Bill it doesn't even exist any longer, but becomes unreasonable conduct.

In 1833 negro slaves in the British Empire were set free. In that same year a Hicktown woman was sold in the market with a halter round her neck. No price was stated, but in 1816 another local woman had been sold in the market for 4s., the equivalent of eight loaves of bread. The nineteenth century was a violent one in Hicktown. Public executions were watched with enjoyment; there were footpads and transportations, fights and strikes. Strike-breakers were put backwards on donkeys and booed through the town. There were poverty and soup kitchens, riots and soldiers with drawn swords charging the people.

My grandfather was born in 1862, and on his marriage became—through his wife—the owner of a public house. My father told me of his own youth in the golden age of Victoria.

"The pub was open from 6 in the morning till 11 at night. Hardly a week went by but my father didn't have to take some man to court for breaking windows and smashing the place up. Every Friday the men would come to the pub straight from work, ready to spend all their wages. But the wives would be waiting, begging their husbands for a little money to buy food for the week . . . When the men got home roaring drunk they would beat up the wives and children . . ."

It was easy to dismiss them as drunken brutes who lived like animals. Wretched ghettoes in alleys were hardly likely to produce delicate, refined people. Many of the children would die anyway from diphtheria or tuberculosis or fever, and many women died in childbirth. Stress is a modern catchword, but to the poor of those days stress was drinking heavily because to think about life was unbearable.

In the thirties, when my memories begin, life was far better than fifty years before, but still rough. Men were on the dole or short time, there was poverty and distress and dirt and disease. Drunks still rolled about the streets, there were fights, and violence in many homes; but no wife left her husband, because she couldn't afford to. There was little work for women in Hicktown, and in most factories they had to leave on marriage, as did our school-teachers—a fact seldom mentioned today when the earlier marriage age is talked about. Then, courtships had to be prolonged, the girls often working for years until they became pregnant.

But there was one little pocket of society, I remember, where there was a different way of life. In the hosiery, tailoring and weaving factories women were allowed to work after marriage, and in the hosiery trade especially wages were high, even in the thirties. There was a strong trade union, to which all the women belonged. In a certain hosiery town where I worked for a spell in one factory just before the war the women were mostly married; they had few children and nice homes. They were intelligent, but would not go into shops or offices because the pay was lower. I never remember hearing of bad husbands or wife-beating among these workers.

After the war Hicktown changed almost overnight. The dirt and distress vanished, as did much of the drunkenness and the cruelty to women. For the women were at work.

Among the working-classes it would seem that cruelty to wives goes on, in the main, where there is poverty and where the wife is a *dependent*, which in practice means when there are young children. Listening to odd remarks from both men and women, it would seem to me that it isn't exactly the fact that there is more money around—though that would remove some of the stress—but that the men *resent* having to support wives at home, even despising them for taking money for services rendered. Both husband and wife have fiercely independent attitudes. "We prefer our own money," the hosiery wives used to say, and as a worker her husband respects her. The working-class women are the descendents of the old peasant communities, later to become the robust brewers and bakers of the Yorkist Age. My great-grandmother was a post-mistress; my grandmother at the pub worked with her husband (and was dead at thirty); my great-aunt was a dressmaker; my mother worked in a weaving factory. My father was a good husband, but he never in all his life told my mother how much he earned. Even though wife and husband worked together, the feudal attitude of the lord and master was still there.

Unhappy people are so because they have been deprived of

love in their childhood, say the experts, as though no other form of deprivation exists. Children can be deprived of equality of opportunity, of any sort of equality—I once knew a little girl who cried because her teacher had said that in his opinion a dustman was the lowest form of life. The child's father was a dustman. Adults can be deprived, too. Men can be deprived of work, of homes. If my husband became embittered and took it out on us, who was to blame? The government?

I have talked to many women whose marriages have broken up, and they all agreed on these points; where there is cruelty the children suffer, but the wives cannot leave while the children are small, for they cannot find homes or jobs. Said one young married woman to me recently, "My father led us a dreadful life, we hated him. But my mother wouldn't leave, though we wanted her to. My two sisters married the first men they met just to get away from home and now they're divorced. I was lucky, I met a man I really loved." Said another, older woman, who had repeated mental breakdowns, "The doctors told me that they were caused by my unhappy childhood. My father used to drink and knock us about, my mother had a hell of a life, but we had to stay with him, we couldn't afford not to."

I didn't want to break up my marriage, but cruelty to the children I could not and would not stand. I tried to do the right thing according to the books, and asked a priest to talk to my husband and myself. This was a mistake, for when one partner brings in an outsider it makes the other partner bitter and resentful, as I was to learn later. It did more harm than good. So I took the children to my parents' home, saw a lawyer, and applied for a separation order. Twice we went to court, but husband didn't turn up. The hearing was postponed again, and I thought I might be joining the ranks of those women who trudge to the courts weekly for maintenance payments which are never paid. There is something particularly humiliating in going cap in hand to court for money from a man who doesn't want to pay. Besides, I didn't have time.

Then a probation officer came to see me, sent by my husband. I was told that my husband wanted me back and was asked about our sex life, which amazed and infuriated me. I thought the question, "Are his sexual demands excessive?" pointless on a cruelty charge. But the insinuation is, of course, that he may not be getting his "rights". I need hardly add that no question was put about the woman's possible desires, demands or "rights". I hate to explode the dearest Freudian theories, but there was nothing wrong with our sex life. But, as Sir Alan Herbert pointed out, all our laws, moral welfare and social security benefits are dependent on the sex theme. Our whole way of life is geared to this, and before an ex-wife can claim social security benefits she must be *pure*.

I had allowed myself to be persuaded to go back, even though the children cried. I regretted going back, for things were far worse. Now there was only bitterness and anger, and I was not forgiven for leaving. But I had been fetched back like the piece of property I was, or that's how it seemed to me. I felt I had no rights, and I was resentful. For the first time I could see clearly how little freedom I, as a married woman without income, had. Even so, for two more years I tried.

When Mervyn (the eldest son, the rival for male supremacy) was beaten, I sent for a doctor and asked his advice. He said see a welfare officer, good morning. I asked the same probation officer to call. He didn't. So we left, this time for good, and I applied straight away for a divorce.

Then I found how little the law cares about cruelty to women, or to children, for that matter. I learned with surprise that at this time—1959—only proved adultery could mean absolute certainty of divorce; as for cruelty or desertion —well, my lawyer almost shrugged. I got the impression that before anyone takes any notice of cruelty to a wife she has to be murdered, when the husband would be charged and the children put in a home.

Another surprising thing which I read in my little red law book was that the law is very class-conscious, and "blows or abuse exchanged between people of culture and refinement are to be more seriously regarded than those which pass between men and women belonging to a less cultivated walk of life ... The parties' social standing and the type of conduct prevailing in the circles in which they moved would still be a very relevant consideration."* That sensitivity increases with money, in short, and the peasant women really enjoy being beaten. "Cruelty is only counted as such if it affects the wife's health," said my lawyer. It appeared that no one would

* *Marriage at Risk* by Michael Benson (Peter Davies, 1958).

believe that cruelty can upset a wife unless a doctor told them so, which meant dragging an often unwilling practitioner to court as well. My G.P. was a Catholic anyway.

The months passed, and there was much correspondence between lawyers. My husband's lawyers wrote such missives as : if I did not claim maintenance for myself their client would not defend the case; or if I did not claim anything for myself and no more than 30s. for each child until the age of 16, with variations on the theme such as separation agreement on the same terms and other terms made by their client; or that their client wished to go to Canada and would I sign permission; and finally, their client would be willing to pay £5 10s. od. maintenance altogether, but he is going into hospital next week, so cannot pay. Which last, said my lawyer grimly, would mean that no court would order much of a payment anyway.

I don't think the new Divorce Reform Bill or the recent Property Act would have made any difference to my case. I had had to leave our house, and couldn't have waited years till I could get to a judge who would decide which of us was to live in it. I needed a house long before then, and had to have the money to put on another. Nowadays a judge can stop a divorce if he is not satisfied the family is provided for. But I was asking for divorce, so there would have been no satisfaction in that. Again, cruelty is not accounted for.

Bill Mortlock writes*, "The new legislation has provided the courts with very extensive powers to reorganise family property and income. The comment of one professional writer is : 'On paper, all these new powers . . . look most impressive. In so many cases in practice there will be no chance to exercise them . . . in most cases the changes would be empty words'."

Two years had passed, while I found jobs and a house and the lawyers kept on writing to each other. Little oddments stick in my mind. The day my lawyer said solemnly, "Will you write on this piece of paper the name of any man you have had intercourse with during the marriage?" Astonished, I wrote "None", and watched him carefully seal the slip of paper into an envelope. I wanted to laugh. During the three long years of waiting I was divided between horror at being tried for the crime of making a mistake, weariness at telling

* *The Inside of Divorce.*

everyone about my sex life for a charge of cruelty, and hilarity at the absurdity of it all.

But the big date was fixed at last and we were told to present ourselves at the Law Courts in May, to give evidence in an undefended suit.

I was nerving myself to go to my trial when exactly one month beforehand I was told that my husband had applied to defend the case. (This was after the Assistance Board had told me I should apply for maintenance for myself, and had been awarded £2.) "I shouldn't think permission will be granted at this stage," said my lawyer, who was getting tired himself of the repeated postponements and arguings. But permission was granted, and we had to start all over again, looking for more evidence about events that had happened more than two years ago, from people who'd forgotten it anyway. I began to take more interest in the law than ever.

Said one lawyer, "So much depends on the judge. Once we had a judge who slept all through the cases, and woke up at the end to give everyone a decree. Another time we had an R.C. who wouldn't give a decree to anyone unless for proved adultery as he couldn't refuse that."

Said my friend Mary, who prides herself on her legal knowledge, "If the cruelty affects the wife's health so much that she has a mental breakdown, the husband will use that against her, saying she was cruel to him. It happened to someone I knew. Her husband's lawyers asked her doctor about it, to use against her, because the doctor's oath of secrecy doesn't apply then."

(This is perfectly true. In English law no privilege at all is attached to any profession except the law itself. Doctors, psychiatrists, marriage guidance counsellors, probation officers can all be compelled to give evidence in court.)

But one happy day, in June of the following year, the moment came: I was to appear before one of her majesty's judges. We walked towards the Law Courts, grey and forbidding in the morning sun. My parents, Mary, and the policeman who had once rescued me when I had been locked out of my own home.

He was a friendly soul, and showed us where we had to go. I said I hoped he didn't mind giving evidence, and he shrugged. "We get a lot of these cases."

(A recent local paper says that an average of ten families

per day ask the police to deal with arguments between husbands and wives or parents and children. Said a police spokesman, "We act as mediator and try to sort out the arguments." It is to the police that ordinary people turn for help, which I think is revealing of the way they want their marriage problems sorted out. The police, although authority, are never quite regarded as Them. You have to watch your step with them, of course, but they are never patronising. And they don't give a damn whether you sleep with your husband or not.)

We entered through a big door and found ourselves among a throng of people, walking hither and thither as though looking for a legal answer to all their problems. Mary said, "Do you know what you've got to say?" I had been given a paper of explanation, but I'd been too bothered to read it, much less study it.

Suddenly a bell rang and everyone stood to attention. Amazed, we wondered what manifestation was to appear before us. A procession entered and walked majestically through the hushed crowd. An acolyte with bell and book but no candle, and a judge, the high-priest of justice. They disappeared into an inner temple.

My lawyer was talking to my husband's lawyer. I said, "They seem friendly."

"What do you expect 'em to do, fight?" growled my father.

My lawyer came to me. Would I like to meet my counsel? I suppose I might as well. We shook hands. We shook hands again when it was all over, and that was the sum total of our legal aid meetings.

My lawyer said to me, "Our case is last for hearing and we certainly won't be heard this morning, perhaps not all the week. You see, these defended cases go on for days, sometimes, and this judge is hard. We'll have to keep coming every day just to see if it can be heard, and then, if not, we'll have to wait until the courts reopen in October. This week is the last of the sessions."

This was something we could not do. My witnesses could not keep travelling twenty miles every day just to wait and see. My mother could not stand the strain, and I didn't think I could.

"Your husband," my lawyer told me, "said that he would

prefer not to defend the suit. He says if you will not claim any maintenance for yourself he will withdraw, and the case can be heard this morning."

All the years of getting evidence, all the worry, the emotional upset of going over all the details . . . writing everything down . . . my mother's tears . . . all for nothing. I might just as well have given in right at the start. I discussed the matter with my party. The policeman said, "If the judge makes an order your husband might not pay. So many men don't." (Of 27,600 Court orders granted in 1958, 18,600 were honoured in part or in full: 9,000 were not honoured at all.)

I told my lawyer I'd accept my husband's bargain, and he told me what I would get—exactly what I was getting now, but divided differently: £1 8s. od. for Mervyn till he was 18, and £2 10s. od. for each of the younger two till they were 18 or left school whichever was the sooner. I asked if, supposing I were desperately hard up in the future, I might re-open the claim again, and my lawyer said I could. But I must have misunderstood him, for in the event I did get desperately hard up, and did ask for it to be re-opened, only to be told I could not.

As soon as I had decided they found out that the case could be heard immediately. We went in.

The judge sat on a raised dais. I wondered what sort of a mood he was in, if he would go to sleep, or if he were an R.C., in which case I might as well go home. As a matter of fact he listened most carefully to the evidence. Nor did he, at the end, give one of those speeches often published in newspapers, airing the judge's opinion of the selfishness/stupidity/badness of one or both parents, which must do more harm to children (who read newspapers, as do their friends) than all the parents' quarrels put together. And it's all a little odd when you think that the law insists that you prove your husband/wife is as bad a person as possible. That's why you're there. Each partner is forced to dredge up every bad happening, every quarrel, all the evil is dwelt upon, the good is interred with the divorce decree. In the fight over money all the happy memories are lost forever.

My name was called. I walked the length of the courtroom, which seemed as long as the Old Bailey. All the lawyers huddled together somewhere at the front, and the judge was perched on his little throne. I saw that I, too, was to be thrust on high as I entered the dock or whatever it was. I looked over a sea of faces, all men, lawyers and barristers, reporters, sightseers behind them—do they come to pass the time of day?—and rows of louts in the gallery. "You may sit down," said the judge, nodding his little head.

I sat down, then had to stand up again to take the oath. The barristers started a lengthy discussion about Rule 14, Section 31a, part of herewith. No wonder the judges go to sleep. Then my barrister told his ludship that I had a prayer that my marriage might be dissolved. So I did have to pray to the judge, that was why they had the bell and book. I nearly got down on my knees.

My barrister asked me a question. "What happened on this night? Speak to the judge, please." There was a silence, while all the audience craned forward.

And every word and thought went out of my head.

The crowds of men looked at me expectantly. "Here, Lord, is this woman . . ." No, I had the wrong scene, I was the innocent party, I just *felt* soiled, being there. The guilty one didn't have to go through all this. The barrister repeated his question, patiently, and I said, "I don't remember."

One of the louts in the gallery tittered, and I trembled. (As one famous Q.C. says, one may wonder why the unhappily married should be tried in public as though they were train robbers.)

"The night when—" prompted my barrister, still patiently, and a clear picture came into my mind. I began to talk, feeling rather like a medieval criminal who was to be beheaded before a gaping crowd.

My head bobbed up and down like a puppet's as I listened to counsel's questions way down below, and talked to the judge, above, left. The judge said once, "Repeat that slowly, please, I must write it down," and I thought of the little juror in *Alice in Wonderland* who couldn't write because someone took his pencil, and wanted to laugh hysterically.

I've often read that undefended cases are heard in ten minutes. I don't know how long I was in the box, but it seemed hours as I went through all my married life before the bored lawyers and the interested gallery looking for tit-bits. Surely, I thought, there must be a better way than this.

My mother was called to give evidence and she stood,

terrified. The policeman was next in the box and he described what happened on the night in question. Then he went back and the judge gave his ruling, that I was to be granted a divorce on the grounds of cruelty. My long ordeal was over. There were to be many more ordeals in the years to come, but I never once regretted my decision. Nor, presumably, did my ex., as he bought another house and married again.

I was given custody of the children and no order of access was made. I did tell them that they could see their father if and when they wished, but I would not have forced them to go if they had not been willing.

I left the court a free woman, with a court order for £6 8s. od. for the three children and nothing for myself. I tossed my head proudly and said that I didn't want *his* money, forgetting for the moment that there were long years ahead when I'd have to care for *his* children, and not be paid for it.

The question of what an ex-wife should live on is a vexed one. After one divorce case two judges summed up as follows: "An innocent wife is generally entitled to be supported at a standard as near as possible to that which she had enjoyed before cohabitation was disrupted by the husband's wrongful conduct. In any case, she ought not to be relegated to a significantly lower standard than that which her husband enjoys. The guilty husband should not live better than the innocent wife. The wife ought not to be forced to have recourse to Social Security benefits unless her husband and his household are also at subsistence level. You are not entitled to throw your wife on to public benefits while you live off private earnings."

And the reality? A National Assistance Board officer wrote to a newspaper, "Very rarely does a court order [magistrate's] exceed the National Assistance scale allowances, even if the woman has had to go home to her mother, thus she is condemned to financial strain and worry from the outset. I have known a woman get an award of £4 a week for herself and child, and had to pay more than £2 a week rent. Her husband, who went off alone because he couldn't afford as much beer as he would like, had at least twice that amount. If he had gone off with another woman the court would have assumed that she had a prior claim to the wife on his funds

and made an even more derisory order. It is a common practice for the fathers to understate their net wages to the Court,
sometimes by considerable amounts, and to adduce numerous
secondary expenses to be met from them. The resultant court
order will reflect these claims without any attempt being
made to have them substantiated. On top of that, if the man
decides to be awkward with his payments, the justice's clerk
will usually refuse to take any enforcement action unless no
payment at all is made by him for four consecutive weeks.
If he remits one week's money every three weeks, all he is
likely to get is a suggestion from the justice's clerk that he seeks
a reduction of the order against him because he can't afford
to keep it up."

"Perhaps," said one famous Q.C., "the real problem of
abandoned wives left in much unhappiness and financial
difficulty might be dealt with by a form of national insurance
which didn't count out their pennies strictly in accordance
with their past matrimonial fidelity. If you can insure against
sickness, why not against the breakdown of marriage?"

When Douglas Houghton was chairman of the Parliamentary Labour party he wrote in a pamphlet, "In the work
I was doing on the review of the social security scheme I
have laid great stress upon those for whom there is little or no
social security. People who are unable to face life with dignity and peace of mind. Separated and divorced wives, for
instance, and unmarried mothers ... I have already given
the figure of 100,000 mothers with young children on supplementary allowances, mostly the women of broken marriages.
Widowhood is a respectable condition (even if she was not living with her husband at the time of his death)—divorce is
not, nor is separation. To be pregnant at the altar is dis-
creetly ignored; if the girl fails to get there in time the full
impact of social disapproval falls upon her. The unmarried
mother, the cohabiting widow, the wife who had reached the
limit of her endurance, all find that moral judgements are
written into the rules of our Welfare State. The social security
of married women, particularly, depends upon a faithful husband or the Supplementary Benefits Commission. This is a
scandalous gap in our social security scheme which must be
remedied. Every woman should have social security in her
own right and be free of the qualifying conditions and hazards
of being dependent upon her husband's contributions. A

separated, deserted or divorced wife should be able to stake a claim to be given the equivalent of widows' benefits. Beveridge did in fact recommend a 'separation benefit' for women whose marriage ended otherwise than by widowhood. Nothing was done about it."

Those who object on moral grounds to the state paying allowances to separated or divorced wives might reflect that Lord Devlin and others have drawn attention to the operation of our tax laws, which enable a very rich man virtually to keep his former wife at state expense. And that Sir Jocelyn (now Lord) Simon, when president of the Divorce Division of the High Court, pointed out in 1964, "The cock bird can feather his nest precisely because he is not required to spend most of his time sitting on it."

But no one can deny that women's status has improved since 1833. We no longer wear halters round our necks.

7

AFFLUENCE

As I sat at the Cafe I said to myself,
They may talk as they please about what they call pelf,
They may sneer as they like about eating and drinking,
But help it I cannot, I cannot help thinking
   How pleasant it is to have money, heigh-ho,
   How pleasant it is to have money.
              —ARTHUR HUGH CLOUGH

MY LIFE WAS not, of course, divided into neat little chapters. I was fighting for jobs, home, divorce, all at the same time. With the divorce over and Mervyn at a special school, I could turn my full attention to my new job, which with its good pay, including paid holidays and for illness, made me feel I was really approaching security.

For an office supervisor an older woman, I found to my surprise, was actually wanted, and my off-handedness in the preliminary stages only added to my prestige. The reason an older woman was necessary, Mr Bacon confided when I was safely in harness, was because none of the men could do a damn thing with the typists.

The former supervisor had been a young girl, moved from the ranks, and quite unable to control her former friends, with the result that about a hundred men, all wanting work done urgently, used to rush into the office, pick out a girl—the best typist—stake their claim, and practically come to blows if anyone else approached. "We're at our wits' end," said Mr Bacon piteously, and from this fate of wistlessness I, the heroine, was to have them all.

I rolled up my sleeves and set to work. A supervisor I had not been before, but, by heaven, I didn't intend to let this £12 a week go lightly. If to put the office on its shaky feet meant reorganising the whole firm, then I would do it. And to this end, the managers told me earnestly, WHATEVER I DID I would have their backing. Ha.

Mr Bacon, my immediate superior, was a nice chap. Looking back, I can find nothing whatsoever to complain of in this paragon. But, like all the managers in the firm, he suffered from one slight disadvantage; he didn't know for two days together which department he would be managing.

The bosses, and there were so many of them, were swopped and changed around with regularity, no one knew why. Sometimes they went to a better job, sometimes to just a different job, sometimes they went out altogether. All the time I worked there I didn't know every bright morning who would be my manager, assistant manager, departmental manager, assistant ditto, top manager, assistant top manager, etc. etc., for the day. I didn't even know them all.

A supervisor has the worst of both worlds. She is distrusted by the girls as being "in" with the bosses, distrusted by the bosses as being one of the girls. She carries the can for both sides.

The girls were a mixed bunch; most were good workers and willing to work; some were not and did not. The work itself was difficult (if you can type in the Midlands you will earn a fortune in London), and some jobs were so rushed and so long that they entailed girls working late and at weekends. They were marvellous about giving up their spare time out of sheer generosity, for much of the overtime pay went in tax.

As on my first day the men came pouring in with their bundles of work, Mr Bacon and I evolved a system. All work must come to me first. I would then sort it out, distribute it in order of immediacy—not too easy, for all jobs were rush jobs—and finally get it typed with the minimum of mistakes, or some outraged clerk (and they all knew how to spell, those men) would hasten back tearing his hair and a strip off me.

As in abilities, so in looks; some of the girls were more equal than others. "Beautiful but dumb" didn't apply to this office, at least, for the girls with the brains were the ones with the good looks too.

Mandy was the belle of the office, and it was she who ended up as secretary to one of the top managers. This happened when nice Mr Bacon had been replaced by Mr Hamm, and the affair was conducted with great protocol—we might have been in the civil service. The top manager told the departmental manager, who told Mr Hamm, who told me, that he would like to interview Mandy. She went along, and the top manager then told the departmental manager who told Mr

Hamm who told me that he would like to interview Juliana.
She went along too.

Then the top manager sent for me direct.

Now this was a grave breach of etiquette, and Mr Hamm
was displeased. But all the T.M. wanted me for was to ask
if Mandy was a good worker. I told him she was a good
worker. Juliana was too, I said. He seemed to prefer Mandy,
and I held my peace.

So Mandy went to the top offices. Juliana was hurt that
she had not been chosen and blamed me, while Esther, who
hadn't even been mentioned, blamed me for not recom-
mending her and gave in her notice. Mr Hamm blamed me
for being sent for by the top manager over his head.

By this time the office was going along fine. I recruited more
girls, choosing only the best, till we really did have a good
staff. In doing so I was making myself easily dispensable, but
this did not occur to the somewhat naive supervisor that I
was. The girls brought all their problems to me, as if I hadn't
enough at home. Esther was breaking her heart because she
was in love with a married man; Betty hadn't paid the instalments on the gas cooker and the man was coming to fetch
it back; the younger ones quarrelled with Mum, and were
more upset about this than today's hard-boiled youngsters are
supposed to be. More often there were legal problems, to do
with women whose husbands had deserted them, and there
was always a high rate of these. Joan's husband not only
deserted her and took all her savings, but robbed her father
too. He was never traced. June's husband also did a moon-
light flit; while Susan's was an on and off affair, one day together, the next apart.

The girl I felt most sorry for was Edna, and it was for this
reason that I let my heart sway my head and gave her the
job in the first place, for she was just a little below our standard, though she soon learned. Her husband had deserted
her and her three toddlers under five; she lived in a damp old
cottage with her widowed mother, who stayed at home to
look after the babies; and they all existed on Edna's £9, less
stoppages, less bus fares . . . She lost quite a bit of time, for the
babies were so often ill with bronchitis; as for Edna herself,
she coughed all day long.

If the Church could see this poor thin creature, I used to
think, so far from condemning divorce and remarriage it

would hasten to find some worthy male who would marry her before she coughed herself into an early grave together with her children. She was such a wilting lily, so unable to cope by herself with life's harshness. I don't mean she was neglectful or inadequate, as poor people are supposed to be in so many letters to newspapers. She was a good worker, but she was not strong. She was, in fact, everything that St Paul would have approved of in a woman—gentle, kind, willing to subject herself to anyone, to love and obey . . . they're just the sort who get deserted, Paul.

My religion had, up till this time, been adequate, if not strong. I had, after all, been brought up to go to church. It was a little disheartening to find that, just when you needed a helping hand so desperately, the Church passed by on the other side. Nor would its Mothers' Union allow you to be a member. When I read in one of their booklets—belonging to my mother—an article about "Louts from Broken Homes", I refused to send my children to church. I felt that, while the mothers were thanking God they were not as other women, my children would be hurt to learn that their mum was in disgrace and not allowed to join a religious sect. So my faith withered away, and my children grew up to be glorious pagans.

The great snag about this job, for me, was the distance away from home. I got up early and woke the children— "Mum whizzes into the bedroom, calls 'Hoy' and whizzes out again," said Philly wonderingly—but I had to leave home at seven o'clock.

I walked across the fields at the back of the house to the main road, went up to the top of the hill, waited for the city bus, jolted for nearly an hour, alighted, caught another bus, jumped off, entered the gates and kept on running, for it was a long way to our office. We had to clock in at 8.30, and every late mark was recorded. The worst was coming home at night, tired, in jam-packed buses, to alight and know I had to walk a mile home, get there at seven or later, and start cooking and working.

I didn't see much of the children, and they were lucky in that they had a second home with their grandparents; if it is true that they needed a stern male hand, grandad was always there.

We had a happy day when the letter came telling me that Phil had passed the 11-plus, and passed for the best local grammar school. He was, in fact, as the headmaster told us at the introductory meeting, one of the cream of Hicktown's children. Phil was a determined child, and I think he'd resolved to be in the cream as soon as he started school. Not for Phil the skim milk of life with its redundancies and dole queues. He was a bright boy.

I was proud. To understand the status of Hicktown's grammar school I must explain that it was as Eton is to the upper classes. The best people went there. It did not mix with secondary moderns, either for games or socially, it played rugger against other grammars and invited the next town's girls' college only to its dances. It was, as a matter of fact, a good school.

So we rejoiced, and for a time life went merrily.

Then I began to realise that Kay was changing. She was being hit by poverty—not hit so much as clobbered. The girls at her secondary modern had as much money as the middle class ones at the private school she had been to before, and she was the only child who couldn't afford things. This is deprivation. She would ask, "Can't we have a television? Everyone else has." Or, "Jane has a new record-player, why can't we?" Soon she began to spend more and more time at Jane's home, with its carpet and three-piece in uncut moquette and its car in the garage.

We struggled on, working and sacrificing in the good old Victorian way. We had no choice. But I began to worry about delinquency. All the articles told me I should, and the statistics printed by experts: "Broken Homes mean Juvenile Delinquency". I know these are intended sincerely, but to be on the receiving end of this sort of propaganda can be very worrying. Why not, I wondered, just for the novelty, print a few statistics about people from broken homes, past or present, who turned out well? Just to give a boost to our egos, which are pretty low to begin with. But right away we'd come up against the sheep and the goats again, and all those who transgress the rules of the Family.

Kay never really understood money. If Jane and Joan and June had money why didn't we? Oh, she knew we didn't have a daddy, and she tried hard to understand, but when Jane and Joan and June flaunted yet another new dress, Kay was hurt. She didn't say she was hurt, she showed defiance. But sometimes I thought I could hear her crying in the little room she'd moved into now the chinchillas had moved out, crying for all the material things that her school-friends had, and without which she felt out of the herd, just as much as Mervyn did because of his poor health.

Mervyn was still at the special school for epileptics, and Phil, as always, was silent. Philly never complained, never grumbled that he had less than any other boy in the form. I thought how well he was taking his deprivation (I under-estimated his intelligence), and waited in fear and trembling for Kay to become a delinquent.

I began to wonder what I could do to help her over her bad patch of discontent. Money-wise, things were easier; I was earning, I was *secure*. The security of having a regular income with insurance stamps covering sickness, unemploy-ment and old-age benefits, instead of a series of poorly paid jobs and a spell on National Assistance, is a feeling similar to that of suddenly reaching a broad, safe path over a deep river, after walking a slippery narrow plank which repeatedly gives way and drops you in the water. Now I could breathe.

The only difficulty was the long journey to work. In the thirties, when all were poor, life was geared to poverty, and buses and trains ran frequently to other towns. Now people travelled in cars, the railway lines closed, bus services dwin-dled. When, in bad weather, the buses were late, Mr Hamm complained. (Some employers won't even take girls who have to travel by bus.) I wondered about getting another house, nearer to my job.

It seemed reasonable enough. My bosses were pleased with the job I did, they had promised I would be on monthly staff soon, and have a rise. And when Kay's teacher com-plained that she was getting in with the wrong type of girl, and when she refused to stay at school because she wanted to earn money, I knew it was time to leave Byfield Road. Kay suffered from a change of environment.

She left school and went to work in one of Hicktown's small offices, and her father's maintenance pay immediately stopped. She had new clothes and begged for a nicer house.

So we went to look for a villa on the road to the city, hoping we'd get one for less than nothing. I couldn't move right into the city, for that would mean that Phil would have to leave his grammar school, and I'd had quite enough school-leaving in my family. The education system operated in such a way that a child leaving the boundary could no longer claim the parish rights, as under the Poor Law of old, and had to claim in a new area. We decided that the devil we knew was better than the one we didn't.

So we searched and saw some wonderful houses, and I sat up at night reckoning what I could afford. How much I'd be able to pay out of my salary—how much the building society repayments would amount to, how much, how much . . .

Every time I saw a house with a for sale notice I went and looked it over. I began to find it all quite enjoyable, this inspecting people's houses, seeing how the others lived. In the end I saw that a new block of houses were to be built in the best end of town, just off Perronporth Road, and these were to cost about £2,800. This price compared favourably with anything I'd seen in the second-hand market, and Perronporth Road was on the way to the city, so I reckoned up more madly than ever. If I sold this house for £1,800, put down £800—could I do that?—let me see, pay off mortgage, £960, yes, I could, I could . . .

I went to see the house, and found nothing but a piece of land. But the land looked well enough; there were trees at the back and not a coal mine in sight. I went to the show house and had a talk with the man, who said that for a deposit of £10 I could reserve a plot. He produced a map and asked me which plot I'd like.

Houses on a map look very different from houses in the air. But I decided to take one of the plots with the trees right behind. They were beautiful trees, and six months later they were all cut down. I paid my money and was handed a document. The house was built and finished completely in a matter of weeks. All I had to do now was pay.

I put my house up for sale and waited anxiously for a buyer. After a time a few people trickled in, dispiritedly, showing no interest whatsoever, who were probably just looking round for the fun of it as I had been doing myself Finally a couple turned up and seemed, from the man's opening sentence—"Could do with a good old decorating"—possible potential buyers. He had been looking at the vinyl covering in the kitchen, which still showed its fading rose proclivities, and the remark is a favourite gambit made when people want you to drop the price. Luckily the chimney wasn't smoking.

At the start I refused to lower, but in the end was forced to let it go for £50 less. No one else made any sort of offer at all.

Then I found I hadn't enough money. I had to pay lawyers and estate agents, and pay back the council improvement grant because I hadn't been in the Byfield Road house for three years: there was not enough to go round. So I borrowed £50 from a money lender in the city, at 48 percent per annum, on the security of the house. I was told I could pay back by instalments if I wished, and thought it might be a good idea, since I should thus keep something in hand. It all sounded so easy, but when I went to the office, where people were queueing up to pay their weekly instalments, I learned what 48 per cent per annum meant—even more interest if paid by instalments. So as soon as I had the payment from my old house I paid off the debt in a lump.

The house grew, and we went to see it again. It was a mews type, which is the modern word for terraced type like the dwellings. It was also open-plan, which meant we didn't have a private front garden. The back and front of the house were almost entirely made of glass, the inner walls—if any—were not bricks and mortar, the ceilings were of plaster-board and the doors were not wood. But they were cheap.

When Hicktown started building houses, as against wattle and daub cottages for the serfs, it had a street of them, all detached, each with a good piece of land at the back. Then the Industrial Revolution came, and while the fields around the town, some of which had been owned by the Church, stood empty, the pieces of land at the backs of the houses were filled with courts of hovels, about ten to the square yard, where people rotted in misery and cholera. In the early twentieth century people grew a little more enlightened and the courts and alleys went—though not till the second world war had they all gone—and the builders went in for ribbon development. In my childhood all the roads were built this way. I was born in such a house, with the front room on the main road, the back overlooking fields, thus getting the best of both worlds. After the second world war, when land became scarce and dear, ribbon development became a dirty word, synonymous with jerry-building, which last is untrue, and estates came into fashion.

An estate is something like the old court system in that

as many houses are put in as small a space as possible. Our builder had a rectangular plot of land, bounded on three sides by Perronporth Road, Shuttle Avenue and a field. Pre-war he would have built one long row of houses on each side of the road. Now he built a sort of maze, with some roads running one way, others branching in opposite directions, and a third set running crosswise between the two, thus ensuring that most houses ran sideways into others and at the back as well, and no one could have more than three square yards of garden. My friends found it almost impossible to negotiate this maze, and one and all greeted me with the words, "I've been going round and round . . ."

The house was also open plan. The Byfield Road house had at least three doors in every room, and in the three-foot-square hall too. We couldn't move for doors. The new house had no doors at all downstairs. This gave us more space. It was also damn cold.

The trouble with this house was that, being so open, we never seemed to be in a house at all, but just part of the street. In fact, it took Gypsy so long to get used to living there that she thought we owned the whole road, and when-ever anyone walked peacefully along to his own home she would rush up and bite him. While indoors we didn't have to run up and down stairs to talk to each other, we could hear perfectly well from any room what was being said in any other part of the house, and next door's too.

As for all the open plan lawns, which we had signed to preserve, they didn't last long as they were. First one man planted a tree, then two trees, and lawns were dug whole-sale. Masses of roses developed in one spot, weeping willows in another. Some owners, objecting to their precious pieces being over-run by children and dogs, put up small fences Soon the open plan estate began to look pretty much the same as any ordinary road in the town.

We moved in and were happy. The house was new, the chimney didn't smoke, there was a fine bathroom with a wash-basin and loo.

Kay was pleased. Now she could invite her friends home. Now she was as good as they. She was happier working, for there are plenty of jobs for fifteen-year-old girls. Later on she was to realise how little she could do without O'levels. Philly, as always, was silent.

Soon I was decorating again. Kay was taking an interest, too, and showed her flair for colour and interior design. She even conquered the staircase by papering it with a long-handled brush.

I was happy in that I would no longer have that long and weary trek to the office. I was happy in my job except that I didn't always see eye to eye with Mr Hamm. This may have been my fault, or again, it may have had something to do with the fact that he knew nothing about the work we did. We disagreed on every point of policy, and this too may have been my fault, for I found that in the fifteen years I hadn't been *working* things had changed.

In the bad old pre-war days life was hard and real and earnest, and people were sacked at the drop of a hat. BUT it had always been the bad workers who were sacked; the good ones had rises and promotions. This didn't happen now, and I checked with other workers in other firms to see if I had things upside-down, as so often I had. "Now," said one disgruntled machine worker, "no matter how hard you work, you don't get on any better," and that just about summed it up. So it resulted in everyone saying *Why work hard?*

In our case at least it had nothing to do with trades unions, for we weren't in a union. It did have something to do with tale-bearing and running to the boss, a game at which men can beat women any day. The Industrial Relations Act doesn't seem to cure anything; now you just get a letter before you're sacked, or so a woman factory worker told me last week, the day after getting the boot.

I thought it might be a good idea to reward the best workers with rises instead of handing them out indiscriminately, which was what seemed to happen—so far as I could see a few names were picked out from time to time, apparently at random, so that some of the few lazy ones would get a rise while the girls who worked really hard got nothing. They complained to me about it and I passed on the complaint to Mr Hamm, together with other complaints, and things grew a little strained. It was the girls versus Mr Hamm, and I was in the middle. I found myself having to take sides, and I took the wrong side, that of the girls.

Some of them left and I recruited more staff, though I was gradually losing the powers Mr Bacon had given me.

Some of the bosses moved, or were sacked, or fought each other, or told tales about each other (we got it from the secretaries) in their aggressive drive to get to the top.

I was safe, I thought. The managers had been so grateful to me for the hard work I put in that they'd called me to the office and told me so. I hadn't had the rise yet and I hadn't been placed on monthly staff, but they'd *promised*. I was going to be loyal to this firm, work for them for ever. One of the reasons I'd moved houses was just to be nearer them.

After paying back the loan from the money-lenders I was flat stony-broke. Nor did I get the promised rise at Christmas. As I sat in the empty house wondering why money didn't grow on trees, I received a letter from the income tax office. Because I had been receiving maintenance payments from my husband for the children I should have been paying tax on these for many a long and weary month. Now I owed £50.

I ran down to see the income tax inspector, and let it be placed on record that of all the officials I saw, and I saw some, the income tax people had the nicest manners. The inspector explained to me that when a man pays on a Court order he is exempted from tax on these payments, so that he is thus better off being divorced than if he lived with his wife and gave her the same money as housekeeping allowance.

In short, the bad husband's tax liability is reduced. Thus, a man who pays his wife £8 a week housekeeping money has to find this out of his taxed income, but if he deserts his wife and children and the allowance is converted into a maintenance payment by a Court order, the Exchequer generously comes to his aid. He loses his personal reliefs for his wife and children, but these are less valuable than his right to deduct the maintenance payment from his income when computing tax liability. The separated husband is thus subsidised, while the divorced wife, innocent or guilty, who receives this maintenance pays tax on it as *unearned income*.

I was now in the super-tax class.

The inspector was very kind, and arranged for me to pay so much a week over a long period. And that was as well, for I discovered, quite abruptly, that I wasn't going to be placed on monthly staff, now or ever. For with no warning at all, on New Year's Eve, while the bells were ringing the old year out, I lost my job.

8

THE GARDEN

A garden is a lovesome thing, God wot :
Rose plot,
Fringed pool,
Ferned grot—

—T. E. BROWN

LOSING MY JOB was a terrific shock. I'd worked so hard, I'd thought I was secure for life. Now I was back in the deep again, with a more expensive house to pay for. I wondered vaguely why women's work is never considered very important to employers, and ran feverishly around looking for something to keep our heads above the murky water of poverty and insecurity. I found a temporary job with a lady who owned a little typing business while I sought for a safe, steady job, if there were any such things.

The way I did get one was fantastic. Ever since I had sent in a short story to our festival of arts and won first prize I had been writing short stories and articles in my spare time. This spare time was mainly at holidays, such as Christmas, when Grandma invited us all to her house. I stayed at home and wrote, which was sheer selfishness on my part. However fond of your children you may be, to spend a couple of days away from them can be heaven. I luxuriated in being alone.

I had sold a few pieces, here and there. So when, quite by chance, I happened to see that the *City Press* required a woman's page writer and journalist, I sent off an article and applied for the job, much as I applied for anything that was going. I wasn't really thinking about it, much less hoping.

I received a telegram, "Please ring me, Editor."

A little appalled, I rang, and he fixed an interview.

As yet, I wasn't too worried. I knew what to expect. Hundreds of applicants, and a polite note saying, "Don't call us, we'll call you."

The *City Press* was a small weekly paper, mostly news

stories and features. I located it in a somewhat tatty little office, and asked the girl on reception if I might see the editor. There were no other applicants waiting, and I grew nervous. They couldn't have taken me seriously.

The girl took me into the editor's office and I faced a pleasant man, who asked me to sit down.

"We liked your article," he said, without preamble. Editors never waste words. "You seem to know just how people feel, and what they say." *I'd had plenty of experience.* "Now, about the job."

I gave a hunted look round the office. *What was I doing here?* I blurted out, "I've never done any newspaper reporting. I don't think—I mean, I haven't any experience . . ." Horrified, I stared at him.

"Well, we'll give you a trial," he said, kindly. "A month, how about that? Oh, and the pay will be £19 per week. Equal pay, you know, for journalism. You work the same hours as men, too."

He didn't ask me, as all business employers did, what I'd do with the children. In journalism, I discovered, there is no such word as can't. One just *does*, never mind how. He didn't raise his eyebrows at the mention of divorce. Perhaps, I thought, this is where I belong, with the raffish crowd of strolling players and the like, the vagabonds, the gypsies. Shakespeare, here I come.

I went out and bought myself a slap-up meal in a restaurant, thinking over the riches that were to come. £19 a *week*. Bliss. I bought the children presents, and went home.

Again we celebrated, and I booked a holiday for us in a caravan in Scotland. Then I started my new job.

I loved the *City Press.* I was at home there. Never mind that I worked hard and had to be out all hours, and the kids were neglected. They didn't mind, I was getting money.

In journalism a woman has equal pay and does equal work. No one ever makes any concessions because she's a woman. If she has children she humps them on her back, or leaves them with mother; no one says, *But you won't be able to work if you have children.* Sometimes I wondered about this, and the modern approach by employers concerning children. Hicktown woman has always worked when she could, on the land, in factories, and she was dreadfully exploited in the servant-class. During the war she was told it was her duty to

work, and though if she had young children she was not
forced into employment, no one tried very hard to keep her
at home, so she left the children with a neighbour while she
worked a capstan lathe in a factory and was paid a man's
wage. After this she refused quietly but firmly to go back to
low-paid skivvying, or cheap, factory-work, to be sacked on
marriage. She knows little of official Women's Lib., but un-
officially she's been liberating herself for quite a time. She is
even getting rebellious, and one sign of this, passed almost
unnoticed, was when a group of women with husbands on
strike took their children to the local Social Security offices and
left them there till they received enough money to feed them.
This, to a woman, is a far higher form of rebellion than
burning a bra.

I learned how to write for newspapers the hard way. "I
want an article about cooking," said the editor to me on the
first morning, and as an afterthought, "Do you know anything about cooking?"

"Not much," I said.

"Go and find out, then," he said. And I did.

I learned about lots of things in the following months.
Trades unions, fears of the workers—even in the sixties they
were afraid of unemployment—big people, little people, slums,
immigrants.

I went to the most amazing places and met the most amazing people. I had lunch with a famous television personality
who must have thought me the biggest nit the provinces had
produced, but I didn't know him for I hadn't a television. I
met a woman who kept a zoo in her garden, a girl who'd
played in a famous dance band. I went on a trip along the
canal with old-age pensioners who were also handicapped,
and came home in tears at their sheer courage and lack of
self-pity, and I swore I'd never grumble again. I did, of
course, just as I went on fighting bureaucracy and injustice.
Maybe I helped them that way, too. I met a couple who
were giving up their lovely home to live in a sun-baked desert
in Africa, where four out of thirteen babies die, and cattle
have no food, and the average age of pupils learning to read
and write is twenty. (Are these the exploiting British? But
maybe the Africans don't want missionaries in any field, any
more than the poor whites in England do.)

I met the children of fatherless families who were sent on

holiday by the W.R.V.S., as otherwise they'd never have one, and was told not to call them under-privileged as it hurt them. I knew and understood that feeling. The sad fact is, though, that by protecting the children the problem is kept hidden.

Journalists were welcomed with open arms by theatrical and dance-hall managers. These gentry all seemed to look alike, being middle-aged and portly, wearing dark suits and smoking cigars. Very friendly they were to us reporters, for publicity is their business. They plied us with free tickets and free drinks and told us they had marvellous stories just begging for a write-up. We took the free tickets and the free drinks and wrote as we pleased.

The *Press* was a bit of a rag, but the so-called sensational stories we printed did far more good than all the welfare societies put together. The poor couple photographed in a tumbledown condemned dwelling were quickly offered a new one by a local council; the child or dog left abandoned was offered half-a-dozen homes. We dealt with all sorts of people and spent hours trying to find out why so-and-so had been turned out/left out/slighted/refused permission. We tackled local councillors and even more important fish in our quest, and often our clients were given what they should have had in the first place without any trouble—thus we had no story.

It is amazing the number of ordinary folk who bring their troubles to the local paper. The paper always tries to help, quite altruistically. I suppose to be a journalist at all one has to be interested in other people, and those peculiar, hard-bitten types written about by some novelists, if they exist, don't work in the provinces.

Some of our visitors weren't always welcomed with open arms, for we weren't as altruistic as all that. The man just out of prison, who walked with an air a duke might envy, annoyed us quite a bit. He complained in outraged accents that the probation office was closed, and he hadn't any money, and where did we think he was going to spend the night? It just wasn't good enough, cried this citizen, who doubtless expected his return to the world to be welcomed with flags and banners. The sub. lent him some money, and we found a wispy-haired lady who ran a prisoners' aid society and was willing and eager to take him under her wing.

I hadn't expected this job to last. Good things never do.

We knew we weren't making much profit, and we had a powerful combine in competition, but we did our best. There were only half-a-dozen of us slapping a paper together every week. One day, quite without warning, the Big Man came to see us, made a little speech, and said the paper was folding the next day.

We sat around miserably, nearly in tears. We had loved our paper. We had been loyal, keen, hard-working, everything that big business tries in vain to get their employees to be. I suppose because we put so much of ourselves into it, it was ours. No one can force these qualities.

So we reporters scattered, most of us to go to other towns. Our cub reporter, who fancied himself as a wit, wrote our destinations on the name-board; next to my name he wrote H.M. Dole.

I trotted to the labour exchange, wishing we still lived in the days when we could be hired out at the local fair. Life must have been just a little bit merrier then—at least you could have a ride on the roundabout when seeking work. The labour exchange told me I must apply for a junior clerk's job, full-time, for £7 a week. In the next queue redundant men were signing on, and no pressure was put on them to take jobs below their well-paid standard. I said I could not afford to keep a family on £7, and I'd been earning £19. They said if I didn't apply for this job I would lose my unemployment benefit, and wasn't I ashamed to be living off the country?

I said no, I had paid my stamps, which was insurance benefit, wasn't it? They said no, unemployment benefit came out of taxes. Different from what I believed; I thought that insurance stamps meant insurance against unemployment, but that's what the man said, though not to the miners.

So I went to the office as ordered, to apply for the junior job. There was a woman boss, who asked me what I'd been doing and earning. I told her.

She looked at me incredulously. "And you want *this*?" she asked.

"No," I said, baldly, "but the labour exchange sent me—"

"Oh, them," she said, with a snort. "Leave it to me."

She wrote on my card that I was not suitable, and I went back to living off the country.

I found my own job, of course. At a local newspaper office,

where I was paid £9 a week for working part-time. And then our thoughts turned to our holiday.

I was learning another lesson about handling money when insecure, something I'd joked about once before when I got the job as supervisor . . . Is anything ever a joke? I had money in my pocket again, and instead of wanting to save I wanted to spend as much as possible. I wanted to forget my upbringing of waste not, want not, and spend, splash . . .

Now I can see how natural it is. If you have been thirsty for hours, when you get to water—or beer—you drink more than if you'd never been thirsty. You need it. If the water dries up you get thirsty again, and so it goes on. When you have a small sufficient supply of water you don't get parched.

I didn't spend it all, of course, except on a holiday which we needed anyway. I didn't get into debt, not ever, but this is another temptation, especially when National Assistance officers later tried to persuade me to owe money to the building society. If I hadn't lived through the thirties I might not have realised how near I was to the slippery slope that leads downwards to the tangled heap at the bottom, where there is no credit, no nice house, no good words from anyone, nothing but scorn and free boots.

We had booked a caravan in Scotland, as these were cheaper at that time, and the scenery was so wonderful. We were going to leave Gypsy with Grandma, who'd agreed to take her provided there was no "bother".

The bother had been over some weeks ago, I told her, and it had been much as usual, Gypsy having a number of visitors looking eagerly through the fence, led by one persistent suitor, a black dog with a white star on his chest, who faithfully stationed himself outside, and stayed, even when the others drifted away. It really is true love, I thought sentimentally, and, "I'm sorry, Gypsy," I said, "but we can't let you go out without supervision."

Three weeks before our holiday Kay said, "Mummy, don't you think Gypsy's getting fat?"

"She's lazy," I said.

"You don't think it could be anything else?" Kay persisted.

I studied Gypsy. She did seem a little rotund.

"It can't be anything," I said. "But I'll take her to the vet, just to make sure . . ."

The vet swung her on the table and made an examination. "She's in pup," he said briefly.

"It's not possible," I said. "She never—"

The vet looked at me as though wondering if he ought to explain the facts of life. "It happens," he said.

I went home and told the depressing news to the children. "When?" asked Kay the practical.

I reckoned up mentally, then got paper and pencil and worked it out more carefully. "No one will believe this co-incidence," I said gloomily, "but it will be the very week we go away."

"What shall we do?" asked Kay.

What indeed? And which of the many visitors had the honour of fathering Gypsy's second family? What sort of mixture would I be trying to foist on an unsuspecting public? At what low price?

"You've blotted your copy-book, Gypsy," I said, hardly, and she yawned without shame.

I knew Grandma couldn't manage now, for she was over seventy. I tried to change the dates of the holiday, but could not. There was nothing for it but to face the expense of leaving her at a kennels.

I tried lots of them, but they weren't interested. At last I found one and went down to see. It was way out in the country, and it was one of the nicest kennels I'd seen. They showed me over the rooms occupied by dogs, and I'd willingly have left the children there. And when they named the fee I could see that we might be having a cheap holiday, but Gypsy wasn't.

So we went on holiday, catching the night train to Glasgow, sleeping on the seats, to be fresh for morning and watch the dawn rise over the Scottish hills. Or rather, the children slept. I worried about that stupid little animal of mine.

We had a wonderful holiday. The caravan was near the beach, and at nights we could lie and listen to the soft splash of the sea. Through the windows we could see the blue mountains, and sunsets running down the sky with crimson and orange and green spilling into one another, and a great red sun dropping into the sea. We went on a ferry boat to Mull, and tasted the soft silence of the Islands. Mervyn was quite well, and we were happy.

We returned on the night train, and again I did not sleep.

It didn't matter, I thought, the next day was Sunday, I could rest all day. We arrived back at the house, and were met almost immediately by Mr Gray from the kennels, with Gypsy and four puppies.

"I'm a little bothered about her," he said. "She seems uneasy. If she doesn't improve I think you should send for the vet."

I thanked him and paid him, made a cup of tea, and surveyed my erring animal I was dead tired.

It was obvious something was wrong. I sent Kay to phone for the vet. He was out. Yes, he'd come later . . .

He arrived in the afternoon, looking as tired as I felt. I banished the children and he examined Gypsy.

Yes, there were still pups, something was blocking . . . Could I hold her?

I held. He pulled. He drew back and wiped sweat from his brow.

"I'm afraid," he said, "I'll have to take her back for an operation. My assistant won't be back till tomorrow. Do you want to come back with me?"

"I'll come," I said, and left Kay in charge of the Sunday meal. Kay would make a good little housewife some day, I mused, the practice she had.

We drove to the surgery, where the vet jumped out, and we went up the steps with me carrying Gypsy. He led me into the operating room.

"Pity, my assistant's off," he said conversationally, as I put Gypsy on the table, wondering if I could go. I had been too tired to wonder why he wanted me to come at all. He moved round the room, making preparations, and with some horror I realised why I had come. I was going to assist at the operation.

"Will you be all right?" the vet asked, as though the matter had just occurred to him, as no doubt it had.

"Yes," I said, weakly.

"It is necessary to save her life."

Frozen with horror and dead on my feet I watched as Gypsy was placed carefully the wrong way up, and the mask placed over her mouth and into my feeble hand. I was to be the anaesthetist.

"Hold it firmly," said the vet. "Keep your eye on that

contraption there. It shows her breathing, which must not stop."

The contraption looked like a cross between a football and a balloon, and was going gently in/out/in/out. I kept my eyes there as he made a cut from end to end in my poor little Gypsy. Glancing sideways at him, I saw that he was pulling organs out, and heavens, there was a pup, and another, and another. The first was dead, the second not fully formed. The vet asked me, as he picked out the third little thing, "Do you want this?"

I thought wildly of five mongrel pups. "No," I said, and he dropped it on the concrete floor.

That was all. He put the organs back. "Are they in the right place?" I asked as he began to sew her up.

"She'll be okay," he said.

The sewing took a long time. My tiredness was making the room sway gently around me. I kept hearing a sound, a tiny, peculiar sound, which nevertheless went on and on. I turned round to see where the sound came from.

"Yes," said the vet, "it's the last pup."

I marvelled. It was alive. After all that, hours of labour, left to lie on a cold, concrete floor . . . He asked, "Do you want it?"

I didn't answer. I didn't, of course. But—

"We work all these hours to save life," murmured the vet to himself.

The poor creature made its pathetic sounds. "I'll take it," I said.

The vet smiled briefly. "I thought you might," he said, and patted Gypsy. "There, she'll do." He picked up the puppy, ran it under a warm tap, and handed it to me. Or tried to hand it to me. I was already holding Gypsy, still muzzy and a dead weight.

"How will you get home?" he asked.

"By bus," I said weakly, wondering how I'd do it. Gypsy was filling my two arms. I just needed another arm, that was it.

"I'll run you home," said the vet.

As we went back he mentioned how many miles he'd done that day. If I felt tired, he looked worn out.

But we all survived, including the vet. And when I had time to look at the puppies I saw they were all black, and each one had a little white star on its chest. Gypsy had had her love affair, but she was never able to have any more puppies. And the black dog with the white star never came again.

Meanwhile time had been passing, as time usually does, and the family was growing up. Kay seemed to be settling down in her job, learning to type in her office. Phil was working hard at his grammar school, and Mervyn came home from his special school. He hadn't, wrote the school, been able to cope with the commercial course. They were sorry but— Mervyn's life always ended in but. Now he had no job, and few prospects of finding one with his poor health.

Lesson ten coming up, another little theory that didn't come off, that there is work for the handicapped. There is a law which is supposed to force employers to take 3 per cent handicapped people, but few of them do this, and no one bothers to enforce this law, or, as far as I know, even to see that it is complied with. No employer is hauled before a court for contempt for disregarding this law. It's just one of those things that don't matter very much. There are a few firms which are really good about taking a percentage of the handicapped, and if I had all their names I'd print them, so that they could get the credit they deserve, but even some of these have a sort of discrimination about the types of handicapped they employ. A man or woman who is only slightly disabled stands a far better chance of being listed as one of the firm's 3 per cent than a badly handicapped person.

Mervyn tried for employment, but no one wanted a person subject to fits. I agree that a fit isn't a pretty sight, but neither is a drunk, yet the first has to be hidden away from the public's tender gaze, while the latter is too common to arouse comment. I am hopeful that now we are being educated by films and TV to see every sort of violence and horror imaginable we shall, just once or twice, see a convulsion, so that we can all get used to the sight, and realise that the person concerned is merely having a little disturbance of his nervous ssytem and looks a bit peculiar, but he'll be all right soon.

Mervyn registered at the labour exchange as a disabled person, where there is a disablement officer to deal with the handicapped. But he never once sent Mervyn to apply for any job. I wrote an article in the local paper, asking other disabled people to tell me their experience. They wrote to me,

and their stories were exactly the same. No jobs. No anything but disillusionment and unhappiness, and the repeated
cry, "If only someone would employ me." Many people refused to register as disabled, knowing they had a better chance
of a job if they hid their handicap.*

The school for the epileptics, where Mervyn had been,
wondered if he might go to a centre. I didn't really know
what to do about this; to me it seemed like putting him in a
home, and permanently.

The problem was settled for a time by Mervyn finding a
job, selling brushes from door to door. He applied for this
telling the manager about his handicap; he was told that
would be all right if he produced a doctor's certificate, stat-
ing he was able to do the job. He asked his G.P., who refused,
saying, "I would not employ an epileptic". So Mervyn applied
to the consultant at the hospital, who supplied the necessary
certificate.

It was a poor job, and Mervyn never made much money,
in fact, most of the time he'd have been far better off on the
dole, but he was pathetically eager to be working. Some days
he was ill and couldn't go out, and when stuff had to be de-
livered I took it round in the evenings. In the end he was
sacked for not selling enough.

It was some time after that we met our first—and only—
local welfare officer. We had been, and were still to be, visited
by many people who said vaguely they were welfare officers
or social workers, all attached to some organisation, often
coming to tell me that I couldn't have something, which
seemed to me to be their only function. If at any time they
did give advice it conflicted with other advice, i.e. health

---

* The Government is now considering paying subsidies to firms
which employ severely disabled people in order to improve their job
prospects. This would mean scrapping the present 3 per cent rule,
which, writes a Social Services correspondent in the *Guardian*, is dis-
regarded by a majority of employers. "A change is also needed because
at least half of eligible disabled people do not put themselves volun-
tarily on the Department of Employment's register because of continuing high unemployment among the known disabled, currently
estimated at about 12 per cent."

With reference to the Chronically Sick and Disabled Persons Act
of 1970, Jack Ashley, M.P. for Stoke on Trent and himself disabled,
opened a debate on a censure motion against the government, saying,
"The Government has failed to ensure full implementation of the Act."

departments said stay at home and look after sick son, Social Security said why don't you go to work? In time they all blurred together in my mind, and it doesn't help matters when so much name-changing goes on. Social work, social security, social services, you begin to wish they'd wear labels "I am for you" or "I am against you". Then you'd know at least which ones to be pleasant to.

Gradually, from painful experience, I learned that there is a ridiculous paradox in the Welfare State. On the one hand there are the social workers from the Health Department and the Social Services, who are trained and whose business it is to get people on their feet again. On the other hand there are the petty officials in the Social Security Department, who are untrained in social work and whose main function seems to be to hand out as little money as possible.

Mr A. (I don't remember his name, we met so many people) was a bona-fide welfare officer. He gave me his card, and told me his job was to visit the handicapped. He was very nice and helpful, so I told him about Mervyn's fruitless search for a job, and his brush-selling efforts.

"Lord," he said. "He's got guts."

"We need them," I said. "Pity we weren't all born in suits of armour too."

"It's a good thing you can laugh," he said, and I looked at him. I wasn't laughing.

"Don't worry," he said. "When the children are grown up they'll be able to help you."

He tried to find Mervyn work, and I was glad to have someone to confide in. Luckily I never grew to depend on him, for he came about three times, then he left the town and I never saw another local welfare officer, not till it was too late. Perhaps they had me labelled, "Not inadequate. Able to stand on own feet."

Mervyn hated to go to the labour exchange; to him it was a disgrace, a reproach, that he should not be working. He had not wanted to leave school but had not dreamed he would find it impossible to get a job. He felt useless, a burden. He didn't tell me this but I saw it in his eyes, as slowly the fact was driven home that no one would ever want him. No one ever had.

And I knew bitterness as I watched him. I remembered the

child he had been, the lovely, laughing boy, the talented one, now the outcast.

He and I turned to the garden for consolation.

I love a beautiful garden, and leaving the large one of the marital home had almost broken my heart. In Byfield Road I never got around to doing much about it although I did plant an almond tree which blossomed in pink splendour in spring, while the children each had a little patch filled with squiggly sorts of plants. The pocket-handkerchief of our new home was just about my size, I thought.

Our builders had taken all the top soil from the garden and carted it away, and if we wanted good honest earth we had to buy it back from them. I couldn't, so we started from scratch.

Scratch was the word. The soil, like all that in the Midlands, was heavy, horrible clay. I realised why there were so many potteries locally; round Hicktown they were always digging up remnants of old sites from Roman times onwards. I could have made pots with my garden soil without bothering to bake them; the sun did that in summer when it dried it all to a hard substance like concrete. In the winter it was a slimy mess which hung on our shoes ten inches thick.

I ordered some cheap "weed-free" turf, and immediately it was down it became covered with dandelions and chickweed. Outside the back door we put down a few slabs, Mervyn and I. These sank at varying angles, making a sort of switch-back set of steps which were all right provided you didn't go out after dark.

Mervyn started digging, but when it was dry the spade wouldn't go in the soil, and when it was wet it wouldn't come out. The garden settled into large lumps, and I went to the market to buy plants.

I put in sweet peas. They died. I planted more. They died. I planted still more. This time they began to grow, but slowly, wearily, as if it was too much effort. What, I wondered, would Mendel, that student of the human race via sweet peas, have made of my row of stunted greenery with—in time—one solitary flower in the middle? That the human race was on its last legs, I should imagine.

Mervyn nailed up two pieces of trellis on the wall at the bottom of the garden. I bought two identical clematis plants from the same grower, and planted them on the same day.

One immediately died. The other shot straight up the trellis, right into the air like Jack's beanstalk. I turned it sideways, not wanting to lose it altogether, and hurriedly nailed in more bits of wood along which it raced like mad.

As gardens go, mine was rough. My flowers spread too far, or not far enough, or grew upside down, or didn't grow at all. It was my fault, I admit, and not Mervyn's. But I never bought anything systematically. I saw some gorgeous flower, bought it and stuck it in the garden, where it had to take its chance. I purchased packets of seeds and put them in too, then forgot where and placed others on top. Gypsy hindered my efforts at every turn. She buried bones next to my Woolworth's camellia, and dug out the roots. She used to eat the pansies, munching away ruminatively like a little black cow. Once she took a violent dislike to the cotoneaster and tried to pull it up with her teeth, but I am pleased to say that it resisted her efforts.

Watching Mervyn in the garden gave me an idea. I had thought before this time that maybe he could train for horticulture, but the Ministry of Labour had refused to train him. So I wrote to the local council offices. They were on the whole sympathetic, for local councils do try to employ the handicapped, but they were worried because they had in the past employed an epileptic boy, and he had gone to the river against the boss's orders, had a fit and drowned. The coroner had, quite unjustly in my opinion, criticized the employers. And to be fair to employers in general, this is one reason they don't want to employ epileptics. If the person dies from a fall due to a fit, they are often held responsible. I suppose sheltered workshops for the handicapped in each town are the only answer if we really want to keep the disabled living at home and make them into happy members of the community; and whether this would cost much more than paying "dole" and Social Security and an even larger sum if they are forced to go into a home I cannot say. It depends on whether we think a person's happiness is worth more than money. Again, the disabled person often has to be put into a home merely because he has nowhere to live. In Hicktown there is a hostel for ex-criminals, but nothing at all for the disabled.

I told the council that I would not in any circumstances blame them if any such terrible accident happened to Mervyn.

This living close to possible tragedy was something I'd learned
to accept long ago, when first I knew what his illness was,
and I struggled to take the consultant's advice and let him live
a normal life. It meant that every time he went out there was
a possibility that he'd come home in an ambulance, or—
which often happened—be taken to hospital. Every time he
was late home I spent many hours of anguish; sometimes I
even went out and rang the local hospital, only to have him
walk in and say he'd been talking to someone. I never told
him of my fears. I kept them to myself, together with the
worries about money and insecurity.

The welfare officer was still visiting us at this time, and he
too asked the council about Mervyn. In the meantime we
found happiness in the garden. Soon we had blackbirds nest-
ing in the clematis. Gypsy sat placidly watching them. Kay
sunbathed on the lawn, Mervyn pulled up weeds, Phil sat
reading social history . . .

While I sought peace in my garden. As if I knew that soon
I'd be needing it.

9

SOCIAL SECURITY (1)

Today, the Welfare State provides many elaborate services—health, housing, education, national assistance, and so on—for those who need them. To secure the provision of these services it has been necessary to confer on the Ministers, that is to say, in practice, on the civil servants in the Ministry in question, very wide powers, the exercise of which may affect large numbers of people in a great variety of ways. How is a balance between fair play for the individual and efficiency of administration to be achieved? What is to happen if the person affected thinks that the Minister had no power to make the order which he made? Or that though he had the necessary power he exercised it improperly in the sense that he was influenced by matters which he ought not to have taken into account? Or again that though he had the necessary powers and was not actuated by improper considerations he reached a decision which an impartial body would consider to be plainly wrong?

With us the position in this field is most unsatisfactory ... The new powers conferred on the executive by statute to enable it to administer the services provided by the "Welfare State" have largely escaped judicial control ... In fact they [the judges] did not realise what was happening until it was too late. When they awoke to it they were at first full of indignation, which found expression in Lord Hewart's book, "The New Despotism", but with the passage of time they became resigned to their own impotence ...

Meanwhile our law of administration, if it can be so called, has developed without regard to any principles. Sometimes the relevant statute provides for decisions on objections being made by an administrative tribunal, which the Minister tends to regard as an appendage of his department. Sometimes it provides for such decisions being made by the Minister in accordance with some defined procedure. Often, however, no procedure whatever is provided for objecting or deciding on objections. The Tribunals of Inquiry Act, 1958, passed as a result of the report of the "Franks" Committee, has done something to improve matters as regards the first two categories. But it remains true to say that over a very wide field the executive is a law unto itself. The only check on maladministration is the fear that some aggrieved individual may be able to complain loudly enough to force the government to appoint an "ad hoc" commission of inquiry with power to examine the departmental files and bring to light such errors in administration—to use a charitable term— as were revealed in the "Crichel Down" case . . .

The French appear to have solved far better than we have the very important problem of bringing the executive in a modern state under effective judicial control.

—SIR GEOFFREY CROSS (now Lord Cross), one of the Justices of Her Majesty's High Court of Justices, from *The English Legal System**

MERVYN WAS A quiet boy. He had few friends, for his circumstances tended to make him shun those fortunate people who were able to work. He did not rebel against the injustices of life, but accepted himself at the world's valuation. He loved poetry and beauty and books, but as time went on he stopped writing poems. Perhaps he hadn't the heart.

He didn't ask much from life. Just to be accepted as the normal human being he was, one who could earn his living. His only ambition was to get a job, any job. Sometimes I thought more care would have been lavished on him had he *not* wanted to work.

Perhaps it was unhappiness as well as the old house with the damp rooms which left its mark. In October 1965 he started coughing. His G.P. said he had a bit of a chest and gave him some brown medicine. At Christmas he went to keep his appointment with the consultant who treated him for the epilepsy, was weighed at hospital, and was found to have lost weight. He didn't see the consultant, but a student. In January he was vomiting regularly and had diarrhoea. The doctor said it was indigestion and gave him a bottle of white mixture. By February the cough was worse and I could hear him from my room, next to the bathroom, coughing and coughing.

Two red spots appeared in his cheeks; he had chest pains and was so emaciated I was frightened. I knew this was T.B., but I thought it couldn't be too bad or the doctor would have found out. When I went into his bedroom in February and saw his body without a shirt I thought he looked exactly like one of the victims of Belsen. I was appalled, and advised him

* Radcliffe and Cross (Butterworth, 1964).

to go to his doctor immediately. He came back with another bottle of brown medicine. I sat down and wrote to the consultant at the hospital who had treated him for epilepsy. He made an appointment for Mervyn to see him, and after waiting for a few weeks he went on March 22nd, and the consultant examined him and sent him for X-ray. Then he waited another week for the result of the X-ray.

In the meantime, my frantic battering at the local authority to get him a job had results, and he was told to start work for the local council works department, on general labouring, and would he start work on Monday, etc.

By this time he was not fit for work. He said he intended to go.

"Mervyn," I begged, "you can't. Not in the state you're in. You just *can't*. Wait for the result of the X-ray. The council will understand."

But Mervyn didn't trust the council to understand. He'd had little reason to trust people in the past, so how was he to know this would be different?

He went to work on the Monday.

I sat by the window for hours waiting for him to come home. At last he came. Sometimes in nightmares I see him now, walking home, staggering, his gaunt body moving slowly as though some force were pulling him back, his ghastly face grey. A neighbour looked out of the window. "My God," she said.

He sat down, and as soon as he could move I got him to bed.

The next day he went for the result of his X-ray. He walked the mile to the hospital for he had no money for a taxi. They brought him home in the ambulance. The driver said, "He walked. He *walked*."

The consultant wanted to see me, urgently. We went back to the hospital, and I was told there was lung trouble, and would I go with him to the chest clinic for which a hurried appointment had been made that day. We went, and I was told that both Mervyn's lungs were affected and possibly his stomach. He had three cavities in his lungs. He was sent to a sanatorium the next morning, and on admittance his temperature was 104 degrees. He was not expected to live. The next week, after hurried X-rays, Phil was in the sanatorium too, having caught the infection from him. Some time later Kay followed. The chest physician said my lungs were affected and advised me to enter a sanatorium also, but I refused, for if I had done so I should have had to give up the house. I could not be ill.

Gypsy and I sat alone in the evenings. I was beginning to feel a cold anger which was deadly, and which Rudyard Kipling would have understood. Perhaps it preserved my sanity. I reported Mervyn's doctor to the local executive council of the National Health Service.

"You know you're wasting your time, don't you?" Mary asked, darkly. "Doctors are never struck off except for feeling a patient's knees."

"People under stress fight," I said. "Did I ever tell you about the doctor my ex-husband told me about? He was summoned to the bedside of a sick baby and refused to go."

"You did not," said Mary. "But it happens in other countries too."

"The baby died. So the father shot the doctor."

"Good grief," said Mary. "You're not thinking of shooting this one, I hope?" (There was no need, as it happened, for he was an old man and he died of natural causes.) "But what happened? Did the father go to prison?"

"Yes."

"Then no one was better off?"

"The next doctor used to visit his patients," I said.

"And is that what you're doing?" Mary asked. "Making a world fit to live in for the next generation?"

"I don't know," I said wearily. "But these are my children, remember?"

"I remember," Mary said, soberly. "So fight on, female of the species. But I still feel you're wasting your time."

"If everyone had your apathy," I began unfairly, but Mary had gone to put the kettle on.

There was much lengthy correspondence between me and the executive council, and this went on for nine months. We all know and deplore the apathy of the general public in England, and one reason may be that no one except a fanatic, a violent believer in human rights or an angry mother has the energy to go on complaining until they are heard.

In June 1966 I was informed that according to the National Health Service (Service Committee and Tribunal), Regulations 1956, my complaint should have been made within six weeks of the date when Dr X last saw Mervyn. I wrote back saying that I could hardly complain until I knew the results of the X-rays, for which Mervyn had had to wait several weeks. The committee had to meet again to discuss this weighty matter, when it was agreed that the delay was due to reasonable cause.

In July a further point arose. Mervyn was by now twenty-one and an adult, therefore I must, if I wished the Council to proceed with the complaint, either let them have a statement signed by Mervyn to the effect that he authorised me to proceed, or a statement to the effect that he was too ill to do so. I provided the statement.

In August I was informed that a particular legal point had to be satisfied, and they were waiting for the doctor.

In October we went back to the time limit, and, as it appeared that the complaint might have been made outside the normal time limits laid down by the regulations, the Medical Service Committee could only proceed with the investigation with the consent of Dr X or of the Ministry of Health. The Medical Defence Union, acting for Dr X, withheld consent and the Council applied to the Minister of Health. Permission from him had now been received. So would I go along to the investigation (oral) in November, and I would perhaps like to know that Dr X would be retiring from practice in December.

As the rule-paper told me that "No person shall be entitled in the capacity of counsel, solicitor or other paid advocate to conduct the case" for me, I wrote to ask why the Medical Defence Union could act for Dr X. I was told that it is permissible for either party to take legal advice *before* a hearing, but neither party may be legally represented *at* the hearing. Unlike Dr X I had no legal advice—I could not afford it.

As a result of representations by Dr X, in October it was decided to postpone the enquiry.

In November I was informed that the hearing would be in December, and this actually took place. I was asked to let them know the names of any witnesses, which somewhat baffled me as I'd received copies of extracts from the National Health Service Tribunal Regulations telling me that "the proceedings at the hearing shall be private and no person shall be admitted". I wrote to ask what they meant and was informed, "I appreciate your difficulty regarding witnesses. The most important witness would, of course, be your son, but if he is still in hospital it would be rather difficult to arrange for him to attend. I doubt very much whether you will be able to persuade one of the hospital doctors who attended Mervyn to give evidence. A copy of the X-ray if you can obtain it might be helpful . . ."

My parents, who had seen the whole thing, could not attend. My mother was ill with the cancer which was to terminate her life quite soon; my father had his hands full in looking after her. I wrote to Dr Y., the physician at the chest clinic, who wrote back saying she could not furnish reports or X-rays except to the appropriate authorities. I wrote to the consultant who had seen Mervyn at the hospital, and he said that he had not been asked to attend the Council meeting or to give a report. It would be difficult for him to attend the meeting, but if the Council wished any report he would be pleased to let them have it, and perhaps I would have a word with the secretary about it. I wrote to the Clerk of the Council who then wrote for a report, but this document was not quoted or shown to me until after the hearing, when I asked for a copy. It stated that the consultant saw Mervyn in March 1966, when he had lost a little weight and had said he had had a "chesty cold" for some time. On examination there was some impaired resonance, particularly over the right upper lobe, where there were increased breath sounds and a few crepitations. A chest X-ray on the same date showed some patchy consolidation in the right upper lobe and also in the left midzone. There was a little fluid at the right base. Appearances were suggestive of tuberculosis infection and sputum examination showed the presence of acid-fast bacilli, and Mervyn was referred to the chest physician, Dr Y.

I went to the enquiry alone, without advice or witnesses. Several people, mostly doctors, sat around the table, I was asked to sit down and the hearing commenced. Dr X. said that when he saw Mervyn he could not tell what he said. I pointed out that Dr X. was very deaf, and said that I should have thought the boy's condition spoke for itself. It did to me.

Dr X. did not say very much, but his aide, the authorised member of the Local Medical Committee, spoke for him. He said that Mervyn was a difficult patient (I'm not sure what that was supposed to prove in an enquiry about the diagnosis of tuberculosis, except that it followed the legal pattern of making the plaintiff a bad character). In January, said Dr

X. he questioned Mervyn about the tablets he took for the epilepsy (he always had to ask Mervyn which tablets he took, as he kept no record), and Mervyn seemed a little confused. I asked him if he was trying to insinuate that because Mervyn was epileptic he was stupid, and if so this was a lie. Mervyn was never confused about the tablets he took, but he was sometimes amused at the fact that he always had to remind the doctor of their names. "What would happen if the patient forgot too?" he asked once.

Dr X. could not remember the visit in February, and he was completely unaware of the symptoms. He produced an X-ray dated *two years previously*, saying that Mervyn's lungs were clear then, and this was counted as evidence. He also brought Mervyn's medical file to the hearing but it was incomplete as to the exact dates when he saw Mervyn, as he had not written down either the dates or the tablets prescribed.

I stated my case, and thought I did pretty well. Certainly the committee seemed to agree with me, and the chairman appeared to take a dim view of the fact that Dr X. had failed to keep records.

Then Dr Y., the chest physician, came in, brought as a witness by Dr X. She said that Mervyn was very ill, wasted and pale. He had tubercular bronchial pneumonia and enteritis ... he was fighting for his life ... One lung was completely wasted. This was the first I'd heard of this, and I was so dreadfully shocked that I nearly died.

Dr. Y. said that she could not hear what Mervyn said. I pointed out that he was near death. She said he was intelligent and likeable but difficult and unco-operative, and his mother was unco-operative. The continual vomiting was not a symptom of tubucular enteritis, so I asked what it was a symptom of. Nerves, perhaps, said Dr. Y., or the epilepsy.

Dr Y. stated that, as a matter of opinion, the tubercular condition flared up within a matter of weeks. The symptoms Mervyn had had before that time, although they were identical, really meant nothing, and an examination of the chest would not have revealed the cavities of the lungs.

Collapse of case. Complaint dismissed.

If I wanted to appeal against the decision I could do so, when both parties would be allowed legal representatives, which I could not afford . . . And there is no legal aid for this.

I suppose it was just a mother's intuition which made me aware that Mervyn had T.B. when it was not medically possible to tell he had it. That was why I sent him to Dr X. that last time, and, when we had no satisfaction, that was why I wrote to the consultant. That was how Mervyn came to be in hospital. Otherwise he would have been dead.

Phil came home after six months and Dr Y. advised me to give up my job to look after him. "You are needed at home," she said, as though I worked for the fun of it. I pointed out there was the little matter of filthy lucre.

"There's National Assistance," she said.

Some people live in this dream world, the world of little children where there is always someone to provide, some charity, some social security to take care of you when you are ill and/or hard up. No one is left to starve these days. How they reconcile this with the slums, the homeless, the child poverty, I honestly don't know.

But I was entering a period which was, financially, the worst I'd yet experienced. I gave up my job and so had nothing, for one gets no insurance benefits if one is not available for work. My insurance stamps were wasted. I had been unable to save, for when I had a good job I always had to replace all those many things which had worn out when I had a poor job or no job. I still had £2 10s. od. from ex-husband for Phil (and I asked lawyers to apply for something for me, but they said husband's lawyers wouldn't agree to it and I didn't insist, for there is a limit to the number of people one can fight at a given time). Mervyn, in hospital, was receiving £1 1s. od. Social Security, and when I asked if he couldn't have a lodging allowance, as I still had to keep the home going, I was told that if he'd been in lodgings he could have had such an allowance; being at home, no. My electricity bill came in and I couldn't pay it. I was frightened.

The Supplementary Benefits Handbook states: "When the Supplementary benefits scheme was introduced in 1966, emphasis was laid on the concept of benefit as a right. This reflected a change as much in social attitude as in purely legal entitlement. It is a change which the Commission whole-heartedly endorsed and wish to foster." So I went to apply for

Social Security, which is our right, our safeguard that we shall not starve. And all that jazz.

Social Security had changed more than its name in Hicktown. There was a new manager, new officials and new premises, one of those lovely large buildings which are built for civil servants everywhere. It seemed to me in the coming months that these officers, as the Board likes to call them, were a vast army of transients, coming and going. You seldom saw the same face twice behind the counter, and the visiting officers also took it in turns, so that I was continually being bombarded by hordes of officials—or so it seemed.

But I went to the office. "Don't forget to touch your forelock," said Mary. The room was drab and dreary, and, for a new room, surprisingly dirty. First of all we had to queue at the desk of the one receptionist. We told her publicly that we had no money and she took down particulars of why we hadn't any money, then said curtly, "Sit down," and we padded to the rows of benches at the side and listened to what the other newcomers said about their circumstances.

I looked at the people around me. Good grief, were these poor creatures the scroungers we read about? Was this old woman, apathetically gazing in front of her, really getting money on false pretences because she was too lazy to work? Would this man with the broken foot drink all his wealth as soon as he was outside the door?

I asked the old woman why she was here. She said wearily, "My husband died, and I don't get a widow's pension. No, I don't know why, they won't tell me. They won't give me Assistance either. No, I don't know why."

"I've been here for three hours," a young woman with three toddlers complained. The toddlers ran around the room and made a noise.

"Keep quiet there," said the receptionist with the granite eyes.

"I can't keep them quiet," the young woman said to me. "They want to go to the toilet and there isn't one here. If I go out they'll perhaps call me. And I won't be here."

I felt like saying, "Let them call and be damned." But I saw her point. "They" might then say, "Come back tomorrow". We really earned our Social Security.

I think I went to sleep. I woke to a commotion. A Scotswoman had entered and was daring to answer back. I looked on with enjoyment. I dearly love a rebel.

The receptionist was very angry. "You'll have to get out of here if you don't mind your tongue," she said, sharp as a whip.

"Oh no, I bloody well won't," said the Scotswoman. "And less of your lip or I'll be over the counter to you."

"Send us more brave souls like this one," I prayed, and looked hopefully at the door, willing it to admit an army of middle-aged, middle-class ladies, brandishing umbrellas, terrible as an army with banners, who would put the petty little dictators to rout once and for all. No one came.

I looked round at the apathetic faces, willing them to stand up and cheer. But they didn't move. They were sunk in apathy. *How long*, I wondered, *before I get like that?*

When I finally went for an "interview" I could not imagine why we'd had to wait so long. A Social Security officer came out of the back room, calling my name and holding my file importantly. I went to the counter, to a niche divided by plywood sheets which prevented you from seeing your neighbour's head but enabled you to hear every word he said.

Particulars were taken down. Someone would call. Good afternoon. It was all so quick that I wondered why these people who walked in and out could not just sit here and interview people as they came in, as the labour exchange did. I realised that the labour exchange was one step higher than the assistance. "Dole" was recognised as a right. "Assistance" wasn't. At least, not by the Assistance people.

During the following period I quarrelled with most of the Social Security officers, and wrote many angry letters to the manager, none of which was answered. I understood the apathy of the claimants now. But I still fought.

I was glad I had the energy to fight. So many couldn't. At least my eyes had been opened. Like the revelations of St John the Divine I saw, not a new heaven, but a sorrowing earth. Women looking after sick husbands, bowed down with care and worry and poverty; women looking after sick parents or children, with no help, no outings, no future except the death of the sick person. And I wondered how they endured it. I saw an old man who cared for his bed-ridden wife, night and day, and when the wife was sent for a week's holiday with the local handicapped people begged to be allowed to go too; he needed a holiday so desperately he was even willing to scrape the money together out of his pension. He was refused, although the coach and boarding-house had empty places.

Another old man who lived alone had a home help, who cleaned his rooms downstairs two mornings a week. Home helps varied, he told me, some would clean windows, some would not, some worked well, some did not. None did any cooking or ironing or washing. When the old man's widowed daughter and her three children visited him for a week his supplementary benefit and home help were immediately stopped. "No home helps if there's a woman in the house," he was told. The daughter had much work and many problems of her own, and now she was faced with another—would she be able to afford to visit her father again? For once she'd gone away this frail, eighty-three-year-old man had to start the—to him—enormous business of getting the help and benefit renewed. He couldn't write very well and he didn't know how to use a phone, so he had to pay the usual long, weary visits to the Social Security and home helps departments, an ordeal for him, after which officials came up and visited him ... all he wanted was to rest and to see his daughter occasionally. But the appalling thing was that the officials were in the right, and no one would stretch a point, ever, in the name of humanity.

I visited Mervyn in the sanatorium seven miles away, on the bus a half-day's journey. I travelled with the wives and mothers of men who had also been treated with bottles of brown medicine till they collapsed at work. "No, we didn't protest," they said. "We know it's no use."

Kathleen Bell, writing in *Tribunals in the Social Services**, asks why so few use the right to appeal to tribunals. The answer is simple. The working classes will, if necessary, take a case to a judge and jury, and feel they have a sporting chance. They have no faith at all in secret tribunals (as in effect these tribunals are). Describing the tribunals in the National Health Service, Kathleen Bell writes, "It is difficult to imagine a system more confusing, tortuous, slow and expensive. Allen states 'It is tribunalism run mad, and it is impossible for layman or lawyer, or indeed medical men, to

*Routledge & Kegan Paul (1969).

resist the belief that it could be greatly simplified with advantage to all.' " In the period that followed, with every
letter I received telling me of a certain decision of Social
Security there was a note advising me that I could, if I didn't
agree with the decision, go before a tribunal. I didn't agree
with most of the decisions, but I didn't go before any more
tribunals.

As Mervyn lay white and still, I cursed myself for not
contacting the consultant sooner. There was no other way of
getting another opinion, for on the National Health you are
not encouraged to change doctors unless you change your
address. If you should want to change, the present doctor's
permission has to be given, and he has to sign the medical
card. You can hardly tell a doctor that you want to go to
his colleague over the way because you feel you'll get better
treatment there.

The sanatorium was a pleasant little place, situated in the
country, and as Mervyn began the long slow journey back
to health he was able to sit outside and drink in God's good
air. There were only two wards, so rules were not too rigid.
But it was badly under-staffed; two sisters and two staff
nurses were the only trained people, and the rest consisted of
"helpers"; married women from homes several miles away,
who came by bus or cycled, as the sanatorium was off the
beaten track. When Mervyn had been there eighteen months
the place was closed down because of an economy drive—
although it was always full—and he was moved to another
hospital in the middle of a town in another county, with no
country gardens to sit in, and so difficult for me to reach by
bus that I could seldom see him. Finally he was discharged,
with his one wasted lung, a cavity in the other, and a patched-
up stomach. And his epilepsy.

During this time we were visited by the petty officials from
the Social Security department. I can call them petty now;
then they were invested with an aura of frightening power.
They were not ordinary people, but dictators who decided
whether I could keep on living. They brought their means
test; they asked to see my bankbook, and every little detail
of any possible thing I had. They asked if I took in lodgers, if
I had any little penny income which they somehow had overlooked. I never went out without feeling They were watching
from every corner. Maybe they are nice people really. But

"there is evidence collected by such organisations as the Child Poverty Action Group, Mothers in Action and Claimants Unions, to suggest that a percentage of claimants have cause to complain of the way they have been handled" (*Birmingham Post*).

I used to lie awake and think about it. I read that an eminent psychologist said that insensitive people become overbearing when given unlimited authority, and that Social Security officers should have a psychological test before being given their jobs to make sure they do not work out hidden grudges on the claimants in their power, or, feeling inadequate, attempt to increase their own efficiency by adhering to rigid rules and developing an authoritarian discipline. And they should, when past this test, have a course in social work.

But because so many of the people they deal with are inarticulate the problem remains hidden, wrapped up in the pretty pink tissue of English kindness. Says the National Assistance Board report, "The quality of a personal service of this kind depends largely on the people who give the service. Notwithstanding the criticisms which have been made of the National Assistance scheme as such, there has been general recognition that the staff have carried out their duties with courtesy, humanity and imagination, and the Board welcomes this opportunity to pay their own tribute to the excellent work they have done."

Recognition by whom? Simply by the Board itself, one imagines, for I can't, offhand, think of any other source of praise. "A Bloody Disgrace" is the *Sunday Mirror's* headline, going on to say, "The most humiliating thing you can do to a man is to destroy his self-respect . . . it is at the glum counters of employment exchanges and social security departments that the last vestige of self-respect can be stripped away by clumsy jacks-in-office who are either heartless, sadistic—or just plain pig-ignorant."

The *Observer's* headline reads, "When Security grows as Cold as Charity", and says, "Even within the rules there is room for more understanding. The department's staff can't become involved in the personal problems of thousands— they would go mad. All one asks is that every single one of them remembers that the citizen on the other side of the counter is a human being, and probably a very vulnerable one, however stupid, awkward or aggressive he or she may seem."

"How the Snoopers Prey" is the *Guardian's* headline on what they call "Men from the Ministry and one deserted wife", while the *Times* asks, "Is officialdom being too suspicious?" and says, "The Citizens Advice Bureau told the Committee [the Fisher Committee] that their experience is that genuine claimants meet an over-suspicious attitude. They reported a lack of sympathetic treatment, especially towards claimants in urgent need, and hardship and distress caused by long queues in dingy offices and delays in receiving money."

Where money is given away we have to have rules. I accept this, but would have felt better if I'd known what the rules were.

The health visitor was a different sort of person altogether. She visited me because we'd had T.B., for with this we suddenly became V.I.P.s. She fought for me against the harsh S.S. officers, and she was a doughty fighter.

We talked about Social Security payments, and about the means tests handed to us before we could claim our "rights". I read books.

"National Assistance is the final safeguard against extreme poverty and starvation, and was only intended for those in extreme need," writes Margaret Wynn.* "Recipients are bound to be subject to an assessment of recourses and needs."

But, "The separated or divorced wife is subject to a more severe means test than she would be as a widow . . . The powers of the Board discriminate between fatherless families in other ways. A widow may receive a grant of 5s. per week towards hire-purchase commitments undertaken before her husband's death if the article is essential, and even a T.V. set may be so regarded for a widow tied to the house by young children. Separated wives are rarely given this help."

This division between the deserving and the undeserving poor is no doubt a very worthy one. Unfortunately it is the undeserving children who suffer.

So with one's basic payment there are also, I came to understand, discretionary benefits.

Discretionary payments are those which you don't know you are entitled to and thus can't ask for; it is all left to the officer's discretion. If he calls and you look clean and well-off

* *Fatherless Families* (Michael Joseph, 1964).

you don't, so claimants say, get on so well as if you're scruffy and don't try.

I knew nothing about discretionary benefits, for no member of the department ever thought to mention this little item to me. No one ever does know very much about the workings of Social Security, certainly not the claimants. If you are lucky enough to meet up with a health visitor, as I did, then she'll put you wise; if not, you could presumably go on for years getting less than your entitlement. Margaret Wynn offers a remedy* : "While the National Assistance Board must have discretionary powers there is some danger of arbitrary treatment dependent upon the personal attitudes of local Boards and their servants. A leaflet addressed to mothers with dependent children explaining clearly what the Board may and will do for them would be valuable."

But much too simple.

My health visitor told me I must ask for extra payment for fuel and for food for ex.-T.B. patients, so I asked S.S. Officer One about this. "You can have 3s. weekly for coal," he said.

I replied, "That won't buy much."

He said, "All right, have 6s."

Some people have a special need of heating during the winter months, e.g. because of ill health or damp and draughty accommodation, and it has been for many years the practice to make an addition to their allowances for this purpose— N.A.B. Report.

I asked how much Mervyn would receive when he came home. Officer Two refused to tell me. I asked about the extra payments for T.B. patients, and was told he would get 12s. 6d. for this. I asked why Phil didn't have this too. There was no reply. Take it or leave it and be thankful.

"The Commission have discretionary powers to adjust awards of supplementary pension and supplementary allowance where there are exceptional circumstances" (Supplementary Benefits Handbook).

Trouble came on when Mervyn was due out of hospital. He had no bed, for he had been sharing with Phil, and the health visitor said this would no longer be wise. The health department had lent us a single bed for Phil, on which the one set of blankets was used. There was no room for a double

* Op. cit.

and single bed, so the health visitor spoke to the S.S. officers and they sent a second-hand single bed for Mervyn. Then I saw S.S. Officer Three and told her I had no bedclothes for the second bed.

"Exceptional needs payments are made for major items of bedding and household equipment where these are necessary . . . required for the first time" (Supplementary Benefits Handbook).

At this time, May 1967, I was receiving a weekly payment of £4 1s. 0d. for myself, plus £3 15s. 9d. for mortgage interest and rates, electricity, coal and all outgoings on the house (this figure included £11 yearly for all repairs, against £20 allowed to council house tenants). I was receiving payment on a High Court order of £2 10s. 0d. from ex-husband for Phil. This was subtracted from my total figure by the Board, and substituted by their own figure of 35s., so the Court order was subsidising Social Security.

I was further allowed another £1, but was never quite sure just what this was for, owing to the habit of various Social Security officers of telling me different things, although they seemed to use the same file. Roughly, I think it was for bus fares for the hospital, and extra nourishment for us all as T.B. patients.

Kay was working and earning £5 gross, so 10s. was stopped from my total for this. (This always happens as soon as a child starts working.) I need hardly say that all my own personal allowances went on the house and the children.

I was sent £7 5s. 0d. to buy a complete set of bedding—pillows, blankets, sheets, bedcover, the lot. I went round all the shops, and priced the cheapest articles as follows:

3 sheets @ 24s. each	£3	12	0
3 blankets @ 30s. each	4	10	0
2 pillows @ 14s 11d each	1	9	10
4 pillowcases @ 2s 11d. each . . .		11	8
	£10	3	6

I checked with the health visitor. She said firmly that I was right. Mervyn was coming out of a very warm sanatorium, and not only did I want the items mentioned but an eiderdown or counterpane too.

I wrote to the S.S. and Officer One visited me. I had, in my letter, explained everything in words of one syllable, even mentioning why I wanted the bedding, and that the health department had lent us one single bed.

Said Officer One, looking at my letter, "That isn't true. The health department did not let you have a bed."

The bed was upstairs, as was the receipt I had signed for it.

He left, and I wrote again. This time I received a letter saying:

"Thank you for your letter. I would like to confirm that the statement regarding the bed made by my officer when she visited you on 1st June 1967 was correct and is still correct according to information supplied to us by the area welfare officer.

"The grant of £7 5 od. was to enable you to purchase the following items of bedding:

2 pairs single sheets . . .	£2	4	0
1 blanket	2	17	6
1 pillow		13	6
1 grey blanket	1	1	6
2 pillow cases		8	0
	£7	4	6

Yours faithfully,
"Social Security."*

I wrote yet again, saying that on the advice of the health visitor I had to inform them that these bedclothes were quite inadequate. I further added that even if they were adequate I knew of no shops where I could buy sheets at that price and never saw *grey blankets*—what were they? Ex-army or something? Second-hand? I said that I would not have my son home until I could care for him properly (I didn't dare), and sent back their order for £7 5s. od. I received a cool letter from the S.S. confirming that their officer's decision was

* Why they added on 6d. was a total mystery.

correct. I knew I had to be wrong, but now the health visitor was wrong too. Mervyn stayed in hospital at a cost to the country of £60 a week. I wrote to my M.P.

My M.P. was a friendly young man. He visited me, heard my life story and went to battle with Social Security. Within a few days I received another letter, enclosing a postal draft for more than the amount I had stipulated.

Strange how M.P.s can change the immovable laws. I bought the bedclothes and Mervyn came home.

The report of the National Assistance Board for the year 1965 says, "Section 2(2) of the Nat. Asst. Act requires the Board to exercise their functions in such manner as shall best promote the welfare of persons affected by the exercise thereof. The Board have always interpreted this requirement as giving them responsibilities of two kinds in the field of welfare. The first is to ensure that in exercising their functions of meeting financial need their officers ensure that allowances are issued promptly and are adequate to meet individual needs.

"The second is to ensure that the officers detect not only the needs which they can meet by way of an addition to the weekly grant but also non-financial needs which are not being met, these can be varied, covering for example the services of a home help, meals on wheels, improved accommodation, etc . . .

"Besides themselves examining the need for welfare services on each visit, the officers take steps to ensure in the case of people who are particularly at risk (e.g. old, disabled, or handicapped people living alone) that a relative or neighbour will notify the Board if some additional help by the Board is needed between visits."

Well, we notified them all right. And the money spent in petrol to drive those Social Security officers' cars up to the house just to tell me I was wrong would have bought ten blankets.

As we had complained to the M.P. we were now dealt with for a time from the area office, which sent a welfare officer (one of theirs, presumably—I never really knew) to see us. His attitude was very different from that of the ordinary officers, and I mentioned to him that I was just a little tired of begging for help which I didn't receive. "You shouldn't have to beg," he said, gently. "But I do," I replied. Surely that was obvious, anyway. I pointed out that I had read the

National Assistance Board report for 1965 where it stated that a T.B. person should have £5 weekly. He said that now National Assistance was Social Security this no longer applied. People didn't have T.B. any more (in theory). He said that if I obtained a doctor's certificate from the chest clinic doctor saying that Mervyn required extra food, he would do something about it. I made an appointment and went to the chest clinic, waited, and saw one of the doctors, who asked, "Why on earth a welfare officer all the way from the area office?"

I said humbly I didn't know, and he snorted and gave me the required certificate, which I duly passed on. But it was the local health department who allowed us the extra milk and eggs and butter which they said we needed, and which were a great help.

After three or four visits from our man from area office we were switched back to the local S.S., and Officer Three called again. (We never knew their names, and they referred to each other importantly as officers. Welfare officers, on the other hand, left cards, and we were encouraged to use their names. The policeman called me madam.) I said, maliciously, "You were quite wrong about the bedding, weren't you?" I was hoping she'd get the sack as if she were in private enterprise.

"No, we weren't wrong," she answered. "There must have been a mistake in pricing. We usually check with the shops every year. May I see the letter we sent you with the prices on?"

I handed her the letter; she read it, and put it in my ever-increasing file. I asked for it back, and it was returned.

At this time I was living on such a tight shoe-string that I feared every moment it might break. Thirty-five shillings was not adequate for Phil, who had grown tremendously; he was 5 feet 8 inches, and terribly thin. I gave him good food, which meant I usually ate little. He was back at school now; and as Mervyn was in bed till lunch-time—it was warmer in bed—I lit a fire only in the early evenings, sitting in the cold in the daytime. New clothes for myself were, of course, out of the question, as were outings, social activities, hairdressers, or anything which might brighten life just a little. I was further hampered by the fact that I had to pay the full mortgage re-payments every week, and I mentioned this to Officer Three, who said, as usual, "You must ask the building society to wait."

I said, "Wait till when?"

"Now Mervyn's out of hospital you'll be able to go to work," she said. "He's quite cured now." But he wasn't cured, he would never be cured.

I pointed out that if I let the house payments run into arrears for six months I'd be evicted. I said that, out of my £8, £6 went on house, coal and light, leaving, apart from the £2 10s. od. family allowance, £2 for food and everything else. Even she looked somewhat taken aback, but she offered no advice on how to manage on this sum. This is one little aspect which is completely left out of the S.S. officers' training. They are told to exercise their functions in such manner as shall best promote the welfare of persons thereof, but ask them how, and they haven't a clue.

"You can't have any more," said the officer. "That's the law."

I said, "Then we'll have to change the law."

This made her angry. "You mean you want the law changed just for you?" she asked, cuttingly.

"For me and thousands of others in the same plight," I replied. "All the fatherless families, for example, shouldn't they have a pension, the same as widows?"

"And who's going to pay for this?" asked the officer, as though it came out of her own purse.

"Who pays the pensions?" I retorted.

"The widows' husbands," said she.

Ah, here was the difference, the holy, social, moral difference between a widow and a divorced woman. I'd been wrong again, it was nothing to do with till death do us part. *The widow had insurance stamp benefit.*

But there seemed to be a flaw in that argument too. "My husband paid insurance," I mentioned. "In fact, he's still paying."

"But not enough for you to get a pension," said the Woman who Knew all the Facts and Figures, and no doubt helped the Chancellor with his budget. "No, it's me who pays these taxes, and I'm sick of it, I'm having to pay more all the time."

"You mean you object to paying to widows and old age pensioners?" I asked.

"For everyone. I have to go to work and earn my money, and I have such a lot stopped in taxes. Then I go out and see the Assistance Board paying out to people—"

"Like me?" I asked. "I went to work too, and paid insurance stamps and income tax. I'll tell you what's wrong with you," I went on, losing my own temper, which didn't take much doing, "you and thousands of the earning, tax-paying, I'm-all-right-Jack public. You're a symptom of the welfare state. You know there are poor and sick and old people—or you should—you know they need money, but you grudge paying it to them, you think someone's getting something for nothing and you can't bear it."

We parted on bad terms, which was not surprising. "This army of civil servants riding around in State-paid cars," I grumbled to Mary. "Telling people they shouldn't have any money, and getting bloody paid for it."

"You're prejudiced," accused Mary.

"Of course I'm prejudiced," I shouted. "I'm a mother; I'm trying to bring up a family including a sick son. Oh," I went on, calming down somewhat, "it just doesn't make sense to me. All this money poured into the Welfare State—or so we're told—and where does it go?"

"Bureaucracy?" asked Mary.

"They say they don't get paid much, these ordinary officials. But at least they have a secure job for life. If they don't believe in the welfare state, why work in a job which deals with the underprivileged? As to bureaucracy, yes, I know it from the inside. During the war, after I'd been working long hours and weekends in an aircraft factory office, I left to have a baby—after I was married, I mean. Then I decided to do a bit more for my country so I went to the labour exchange and asked for a job. They sent me into the Civil Service, which needed a clerk. When the manager learned I could type he employed me as an extra and unnecessary typist and started another clerk. I worked there till I couldn't stand it any longer, doing less work in less hours than ever before or since. And there was a war on. That's God's truth, and I was disgusted."

Life went on in a dreary sort of way. We got up, we ate, after a fashion, we went to bed, we slept, coats over our thin blankets. We didn't laugh so much. We were cold in winter because we couldn't have too big a fire, we didn't really have enough to eat and cheap meals are seldom nutritious, although I knew all about herrings and breast of lamb. In fact, I used to go the the butcher's and ask for a cheap breast of lamb for the dog, take it home and stew it; we ate the meat, Gypsy had the bones. Even she looked disgruntled. We went back to nettles and dandelion leaves and blackberries, in season. My old age pensioner parents often fed the children.

Phil studied for his O-levels, and he was forced to do so in the open-plan lounge, as there was no chance of heating the bedroom he shared with Mervyn, who was often ill anyway. We huddled round the coal fire and wished we were rich.

Kay started going out in the evening. She was beginning to get dissatisfied. She said one day, "I shall never marry a poor man."

"I suppose I can't blame you," I said.

"I want to go to London," she added.

My children were growing up. "Why London?" I asked.

"To make money," said Kay. Strange how when you have no money you think of little else. You dream of pennies floating through the air, you reach out to grasp them and you wake up.

"Sue's gone, and Jane," Kay was saying, "and there's lots of work and plenty of money. I'm eighteen and I get £5 10s. od. here in Hicktown."

Phil said, "I'm getting out just as soon as I've passed my A-levels. Unless you want me to stay and work."

"No," I told him, "you must do as *you* want." On this I was determined. I looked at my usually silent son and asked, "What *do* you want to do?"

"Start a revolution," he said, simply.

I stared at my baby as a hen must when her young rooster begins to crow, and wondered fleetingly if I should have taught him to accept meekly the state of life in which it had pleased God and the divorce court and the Social Security board to place him.

He said, "I'm a socialist. But the present system must go. No more parasites, priests, capitalists, civil servants . . ."

"Who's going to run the country, then?" I asked.

"We could try government of the people by the people. Don't get me wrong, I'm not a communist. But I don't believe that middle-class bureaucracy is true socialism, it's just a bourgeois take-over."

"Many people are better off than before the war," I said.

"Are you?"

"No."

"I've read *1984*," said Phil. "Our danger is the propaganda put out which makes everyone believe that the workers are scroungers, spendthrifts, asking for too much money . . . Going to the doctor for cotton wool . . . Do you know how much income tax relief a doctor gets? . . . And the official is always right. The proles always wrong."

"We are free to say what we think," said Kay.

"We have tribunals in fr. dom, and we're proved wrong."

"1984 is on the way," said Kay.

"It's here now," said Phil. "Comrades, never have our children been so bonny, never have so many houses been built, never have we had it so good. Our statistics prove this, our figures . . . I've been looking up a few figures, trying to find out how much is paid out to officials in the inner party compared with benefits paid to fatherless families and so on, the sick and disabled, men without work. I found this to be going on with . . ." He reached down his old satchel, tied up with string, and pulled out a newspaper cutting. "A *Sunday Times* report," he said, "called 'The Secret Machinery of the Poverty Code—the hidden power of Bureaucracy'."

I began reading.

"The biggest growth point in the supplementary benefits industry is the campaign to track down 'frauds'. Over 100 pages of the AX code—a document unknown outside the Ministry—lay down the rules for this. The most sensitive parts deal with the work of special Investigators, whose job is secretly to collect evidence of fraud . . . Paragraph 2109 of the AX code flatly contradicts the concept that a man is innocent until proved guilty . . .

"The job of 'resolving' the problem rests with the Fraud Officers in each local office, or with the roving 'élite', the Special Investigators. Under the Labour government the number of SIs doubled to 196, under the Conservatives growth has been even faster; there are now 270, costing almost £1 million a year."

"One million pounds a year for secret police," said Phil.

I read on.

"The official most immediately concerned is the Fraud Officer; there are normally one or two of these at each of the 986 local Social Security offices. A Fraud Officer is supposed to receive a week's intensive training. In practice, it is common for someone to fill the post at one or two days' notice. As with other parts of the supplementary benefits system, decisions vital to a family's future are being made every day by officials lacking even the qualifications which, at a national level, the Supplementary Benefits Commission considers necessary. The SIs, who work out of the regional offices, have more power. An SI seeking evidence of fraud acts like a policeman, prosecutor and jury ... The Ministry assured us last week 'the SI informs the claimant of all the evidence against him or her which might be used to establish fraud or overpayment'. Section 8 or paragraph 2493 shows that this is not always so."

I said, "Are you sure this is about England?"

"Land of the free," said Phil. "Oh, come off it, Ma, you're a prole yourself, don't make out you're surprised."

"Just surprised to see it written," I said, and read on :

"The Department of Health and Social Security denies that there is any such official classification as 'work-shy'. Yet the documents photographed above show that it is enshrined in a printed form—and an untrained official can classify a man as 'work-shy' on his first application for benefit."

"And then," Phil went on, "while so much propaganda is given out about scroungers on Social Security, little is said about other methods of fraud. I have here," he dived into his satchel again, "a *Sunday Times* report which says that abuse is not tied to the poverty line. It's by Michael Meacher, who's Labour M.P. for Oldham West." He began to read.

"For by restricting the terms of reference of their new Committee of Inquiry to social security, the Government has precluded attention being drawn to other areas where abuse is a far more lucrative occupation, such as Tax evasion. In a decade 113,161 persons were forced to hand over £152,577,038 after evading taxes. Since less than a third of this total was accounted for by penalties, including interest, the remainder demonstrates the scale of the abuse involved, amounting to an average of £930 per individual. Yet the number of criminal proceedings entered into on these grounds totalled only 1,240 for the decade. Nearly ten million pounds is written off as irrecoverable, while the proportion of each year's total accounted for by the taxpayer having gone abroad or become untraceable rose from 16 per cent to 45 per cent. For estate duty alone detected cases during a decade number 1,240, involving sums totalling £1,545,159, yet only five prosecutions were made."

"Go on," I said.

"Abuse exists in the field of Social Security on a frankly miniscule scale," Phil continued, still quoting. "In a most thorough survey of 32,000 men and women interviewed, who had been unemployed for two years or more and drew National Assistance, only 7 per cent were considered 'work-shy', and of these three-fifths were physically or mentally handicapped."

"Like Mervyn," I said.

"Prosecutions for fraud involving *all kinds* of benefit during the year were only 7,244 out of 23,600,000 claims. This amounts to a fraud level of one-fortieth of one per cent."

Phil put his papers down. "So do you wonder I get angry?" he asked. "It's time someone did."

"Is it yourself you're angry about?" I asked.

"Oh no," said Phil. "I'm all right. I'm the cream, remember? I'm the one the country wants, to work for it, and if a war comes to fight for it."

"I was important in the last war, I seem to remember," I said.

"Ah, but you're not needed now, are you? And Mervyn . . . the country can afford to treat Mervyn shabbily, he can't work very well, can't fight. Might as well put him in a gas-chamber and be done with it. But then," his eyes were suddenly hard, "they needn't come knocking on my door when they need young men."

So our years of poverty had had an effect. On me, too. A more serious tone entered into our lives from that moment. Spurred on by Phil we spent long hours discussing social history, complacency in Britain which keeps the greatest problems hidden—"It can't happen here", "No one starves these days"—until a body such as the Child Poverty Action Group suddenly discloses heart-rending figures, or an M.P. raises a plaintive voice about fatherless families, or a television programme shows us the homeless. We stopped laughing. We didn't have much to laugh about. But I had been fired with something, burning zeal, perhaps. I started looking into things, writing around, joining women's clubs as long as they didn't ask for a big subscription. I became a member of the Married Women's Association, open to all women, married or single, whose chief work is to obtain equal financial partnership in marriage. I sought other fatherless families and came up with some interesting information.

Letter: "I live in an area that has the most difficult National Assistance Board that any person has ever come across. I have had as little as 2s. and been refused help. Recently I have been in the red on my rent, £10, and an officer came to see me and said I must not misappropriate government money, if I continued to do so they would take my allowance off me and I would have to go to the office to collect it. Which is seven miles away. I have seven children under 14, and they are well fed and have 100 per cent school attendance—Deserted Wife."

What the point would be of making this woman walk seven miles for her payments I cannot imagine. Punishment for being poor seems to be a peculiarly English institution.

Letter: "I was a widow who remarried. After 6 months my husband told me to get out of our rented flat. I applied for maintenance, but the case was dismissed. I've used all my savings, now I've nothing left. My commitments are £5 3s. od., the N.A.B. gives me £3 19s. od. The worry of how to survive has reduced me to a physical wreck."

Supplementary Benefits Handbook introduction: "*It is, of course, important to foster and build up the self-respect of the people who come to the Commission, and their liberty of action and independence have to be respected.*"

A Medical Officer wrote: "I would be horrified with this if I were not dealing with this type of problem so often. It is not at all as uncommon as the average reader may think."

Wrote Margaret Wynn in *Fatherless Families*: "A mother who has been granted 15s. for food by a voluntary body may find that when she applies for a weekly addition or a discretionary grant she is told that she already has an extra 15s. and so should be able to manage without it. The voluntary society is not subsidising the mother, but the National Assistance Board."

A president of the W.R.V.S.: "Every year we send children for free holidays, often having to give them clothes first. They are almost always the children of mothers on their own—usually separated or divorced. This class is, without exception, the poorest in the country."

Letter: "My husband disappeared and my 19-year-old son and I made our home with two old people who are both in ill health, and have come to rely on me for moral and practical support. I get no maintenance. My son was ill for five months with virus pneumonia, but nevertheless the National Assistance Board insisted that I must still register for work. Fortunately they didn't find a job for me till my son was better. The officer of the Ministry argued very belligerently and in a bullying way that two old ill people and a sick son was no reason why I should not work from 7 a.m. to 5.30 p.m. He said, 'I resent paying taxes to keep people like you.' I was sent to an ordnance factory 15 miles from my home. I am a social worker by training and said that I was not suited to the job and could not leave my son for such a long period. The Labour Exchange disqualified me from receiving any benefit for five weeks. I am quite destitute." (This woman's doctor wrote to the labour exchange.)

"No old age pensioner faces the loneliness and poverty of divorced and separated women," the letter continued. "They can apply for National Assistance, but they are supposed to register for work. When the children are 15 they are forced to do so, and they must take any work offered to them. As soon as a child starts to work the rental grant is cut. The more adult and conscientious the woman the greater the burden she is forced to carry. I have seen slovenly hopeless types get away with help I would not dare ask for."

I pondered the last words of the letter. The Way to Get on when Poor, or How to Become a Scrounger in Six Easy Lessons. Touch your forelock, cringe, and forget all about self-respect and simple dignity. Human nature will do the rest. We'll give you more if we can scorn you and despise you and fuss you and teach you how to be self-respecting again. We just can't bear you to be defiant. All right, I thought, cringe I won't, but I will try asking without fawning.

So when Officer Three called on her periodic visit to carry out her *"statutory duty to promote the welfare of people receiving assistance, and to identify needs requiring reference to other agencies and other special action"* (Report of the National Assistance Board) I asked, like Oliver Twist, for more. The Supplementary Benefits Handbook says: *"If a recipient of Supplementary Benefit is responsible for internal decoration of his accommodation, an exceptional needs payment may be made to meet the cost of essential redecoration. Where the labour is provided by a voluntary body a pay-*

ment may be made for the cost of materials." So I asked about help for my decorating, as the deeds of my house said that I had to keep it in good repair.

"No," said Officer Three. "Help for decorating is only given to people in council houses."

I asked about insurance stamps, a big worry to me since I had had to give up working. I had previously asked Officer One about this. "You'll have credits," he said, so I stopped worrying.

Then the Ministry of Pensions wrote to ask why I had no stamps, pointing out that I could be prosecuted for this. I rushed down to see them about my credits. "No, no," they said, "you have no credits. Either you buy a non-employed stamp or you apply for non-payment, but we don't advise the latter, for this will mean you will lose *all* benefits, including part of the old age pension," and they gave me lots and lots of leaflets.

I read all the leaflets, but none told me what I wanted to know. I wrote to the head office, thinking that somewhere there must be a person who could answer my question, namely, "If I had ten years' benefits from ex-husband's stamps till the divorce, and twenty years after that with few stamps, should I get *any* pension at all, and if so, how many pennies?" They wrote back to say they couldn't tell me.

"Go and ask your Ministry," they tell us, and every Ministry prints thousands of little leaflets which they give to you by the dozen. But ask them a straightforward question which isn't answered in the leaflets and just try to get an answer. All Ministries dealing with Social Security seemed to have a horror of putting anything in writing, apart from the said official leaflets, which usually are no help.

Finally I asked Officer Three, to see what interpretation she would put on my insurance stamps and old age pension rights. (Again it is a singular beauty of Ministry officials, and possibly why they hesitate to put anything in writing, that each puts a different interpretation on any one given subject. I had already been given three answers, yes, no, don't know.)

Officer Three was firm. "No credits."

I said, "So I lose my old-age pension?"

She shrugged.

"So what happens?" I persisted.

"You'll have to come to us," she said.

"God forbid," I said piously.

Who can realise the importance of insurance stamps?

I asked about clothing and footwear for myself. "*The replacement of clothing and footwear is a recurring and continuing living expense which is provided for in the supplementary benefit scale rate* (sic). *It is therefore only where there is some exceptional circumstance that additional help by means of a lump-sum payment can be made—for example, where an individual or a family, without reserves of capital, has been living at or below supplementary benefit levels for some time. Where there has been failure to provide for replacements from income it may still be necessary to award a lump-sum to meet an immediate need*" (Supplementary Benefits Handbook).

The officer said no. Mervyn was in fact given a small grant, but not the old floor-scrubber, not the king-pin of the home, as the health visitor put it, the one who keeps the family going.

"It's the law," the officer said.

"What about this bit M.P.s are always quoting?" I asked her. "About each case being judged on individual merits?"

"That isn't true," said the officer. "This is the law, and I know the law, and I've had orders from area office." She was always getting orders from area office about us.

"Can't I have anything?" I asked plaintively.

She studied my file. "You've had a bed," she said.

I had indeed, a dreadful old second-hand bed in terrible condition. I had often wondered where it had been obtained —salvaged from a rubbish tip? I saw later an advert in the local paper. "Your old bed *in any condition* in part-exchange. We have an arrangement with Social Security to provide them with beds."

"You had bedding," pursued the officer.

"After my M.P. forced your hand."

"And," she continued, "we once paid your electricity bill, just after you went on holiday."

"Say that again."

"You'd just been on holiday, and then we paid your electricity bill. It's down here in your file."

I was dumbfounded. "When I went on holiday I was working," I said. "Long before you paid that bill."

She didn't flicker an eyelid. "It's down here," she repeated, as though it had been written in letters of fire by an angel.

I was alarmed. If I make false statements to the Board, it is an offence. But supposing the Board makes a mistake, can I prosecute them?

I remember reading about a meeting of health visitors who had said that the Ministry of Social Security was "all shrouded in mystery". They had said, "We must get tough with authority."

But how can you get tough with mystery?

So the bit in the Supplementary Benefits Handbook about claimants having a right to courtesy and understanding didn't seem to apply to us. We had no rights, and there was a law that said so.

Then Officer Three went on holiday or somewhere, I hoped she'd emigrated, and Officer Four called. This was the nicest officer of them all and we had no argument, just talked about the weather. I didn't even bother to ask for anything else. He rose to go.

Gypsy knew all about my troubles with the Board, of course, and in her typically muddled and confused way got it all mixed up. On his way out she ran and bit the Nice Man's ankle.

I hastened to apologise, not wanting to be prosecuted too, but he was nice about it and said there was no damage done. Merely a thread pulled in his trousers.

And when the next visitor called, Officer One, I asked about the accident. "It was all right," he said. "He had a new pair of trousers through Social Security."

I'm glad someone gets discretionary benefits.

10

SOCIAL SECURITY (2)

The Poor Law Report of 1834 did not give, and no one asked for, a supplementary inquiry into the causes of unemployment and poverty, nor for a classification of the thousands of men, women and children to whom the Report referred to as paupers ... Subsequent experience proved this lack of classification to have been a profound error. There were many kinds of paupers, among whom the sick, infirm, imbecile, orphans, infants in arms and widows predominated. Able-bodied men and women were in a minority.

In 1871 the Poor Law, public health and the small Local Government Act Department were brought together under one Minister as the Local Government Board. But the Act then departed from the Commissioners' explicit recommendation that there should be one Permanent Secretary responsible for Poor Law and one responsible for public health ... The emphasis of long practice, the natural bent of public opinion and the Parliamentary mind was on the Poor Law and Poor Law methods, on deterrence rather than prevention, on relieving destitution rather than preventing disease, on organising work-houses rather than clearing slums. As a consequence public health found itself subject to Poor Law methods. Poor Law inspectors became general inspectors without the requisite medical knowledge.

—*A Social and Economic History of Britain*
by Pauline Gregg (Harrap & Co., 1964)

ENGLAND IS A land of tradition, and the tradition of the undeserving poor dies hard. One hundred years after the Local Government Board was set up, ill-health is still one of the main causes of poverty, and still the Health Departments and doctors wage an often losing battle with the Poor Law Guardians, I beg their pardon, National Assistance, that is, the Department of Health and Social Security. Oh, what's in a name, a rose by any other name still smells ...

At this period I made a vow. I swore that my family would never go hungry again. Not if I stole, not if I took to prostitution—if I wasn't too old ...

"My dear girl," Mary said, "you can't be a prostitute on Social Security. You can't even do it for free on Social Security, or you'll have Special Investigators standing outside your door day and night. They'll say he's supporting you. No love life for you, girl."

"You wouldn't be pulling my leg, would you?" I asked.

"Take a look at this, I brought it to show you." She thrust a newspaper under my nose, and I read about the founding of the Birmingham Claimants' Union, one of the first in the country, formed by a middle-class young woman who'd had to apply for Social Security, and been appalled at what she found. The Union was started, she said, because "for every scrounger there must be at least ten people who are not getting what they are entitled to," and, at present, discretion depends entirely on the officer dealing with a particular case, on his asking the appropriate questions or seeing the right things during a home visit, and, further, that because claimants do not know the rules they cannot point out something which the officer has overlooked.

"Interesting," I said, and read on about the unmarried mother who was told pointedly by one officer, "Personally, I don't think you should get a penny, you should be out working."

"That sounds familiar," I said. "They do all go to the same school."

"Read this about men friends," and Mary pointed.

"One of the most frequent questions put to deserted wives is: 'Who was the man you were seen with?' Any man seen calling regularly, or going out with the woman, is assumed to be cohabiting with her. This, in the eyes of the Social Security, means he is supporting her, and her book is withdrawn at once. Often you have to choose between boy friends and Social Security. They go to immense lengths to find out what is happening, calling at 7.30 in the morning, standing outside the house to see who is going in and out..."

(Since that was written questions have been asked in Parliament about the paid army of snoopers, who not only ask intimate details of divorced women about their private lives but ask neighbours, landlords and employers, and even children.)

"Snooping," Mary said. "They get paid for it, you know. Out of our taxes. Wouldn't you like a job like that?"

"No," I said.

Mary changed the subject. "How's Kay now?"

"Getting on well enough. Though—she wants to go to London. And she's right, I've been thinking about it. She must get out of Hicktown."

Mary looked at me.

"We are now," I said, "at the point of judging what effect our years of hardship have had on the kids. Mervyn is still ill. Phil's been turned into a militant socialist. And Kay is out for money."

"That's why she insisted on leaving school at fifteen."

"Yes. She's really suffered. I've thought about it," I went on. "She's an intelligent kid, she must have her chance."

"And you?" Mary asked. "What about your chance?"

"You mean *when the children go to work they'll be able to help you, mother?* Supposing they do, and I keep them at home to help support us, as was always done in the past. And they're filled with bottled-up resentment and move from one poor job to another because of this, then they get married just to get away, and so we all stay poor for life. Oh no, I never intended this. My mother's generation was the last to sacrifice the children for the family, just as her mother's was the last generation to have big families."

"Is that so?"

"Yes, my mother told me once that women said, after the first world war, they'd never have lots of children again. I don't know any more about it, but I do know that in my childhood big families were an exception, not the rule."

"You could be right," Mary said. "So Phil will go to university?"

"Yes. Mind you, I feel bloody guilty every time I look into the S.S. officer's accusing eyes. *Wanting more off the State, Mrs Colin?* It would make such a cosy, happy ending, wouldn't it? Children working their little fingers to the bone to help. You could almost say it was their duty. I don't think it is. Why should they ruin their lives too?"

"So that will leave you and Mervyn. But how on earth are you going to manage, all the years ahead? I don't know how you've managed up to now."

"It usen't to be so bad," I said. "When Mervyn was younger my parents helped out. That's why I could work. Now—" my mother was dead, my father was old. Old and alone, and I couldn't help him, either. Yet my mother must have realised this would happen when she'd decided, all those years ago, not to have a big family. She, the suffragette, must have known that that was the end of family help. She must have known that it would mean hardship in the beginning. They started women's lib., really, all those working-class wives who refused to have too many babies, and broke up once and for all the family as a free-help society.

But you still had to look after your children. They were your responsibility. And you owed just as much to the healthy ones as the sick one, they had their rights too.

It wouldn't be easy, for Mervyn couldn't be left alone all day, not now, he might have one of his attacks. I'd never felt able to go out since I found him lying on the floor in a pool of blood with a broken nose . . . It had been Saturday, the doctors' day off, and the only one of the four partners on duty was out. His wife had called an ambulance and we'd gone to the hospital out-patients, crowded with youngsters with cuts and bruises all here because they couldn't get a doctor . . . Mervyn had more serious attacks than this, he burned his arm, cut his mouth badly . . . he had no warning of the attacks, just fell like a log . . . once at my father's he fell on the open fire . . .

"They must go," I repeated. "But—I'm not sacrificing Mervyn, am I?"

"Sacrificing yourself," Mary said, shortly. "Why is a mother always supposed to be sacrificed anyway?"

"Because no one else would be so daft as to do it," I said, and we laughed. "Oh, I can stand the illness, I can stand the poverty; what I cannot stand is being treated as a scrounger. I don't think I'm over-sensitive, I must have the hide of a rhinoceros to put up with some of the things said to me. Besides, it isn't only me, I've found that out. *'Why don't people claim what they're entitled to?'* " I mimicked. "Because when they ask, they're refused, that's why. And that goes for old age pensioners too."

"What you need," Mary advised, "failing a private income, is a job with such good pay that you could afford to hire a nurse."

"Yes, indeed," and I picked up a national newspaper. "Something in my simple line, not needing too many qualifications."

"Here you are, just the job. Social Security research, salary £2,318. You wouldn't need to do any research, would you?"

Together we bent over the ad. Qualifications 1st or 2nd class honours degree, or post-graduate degree in operational research, social administration, sociology, statistics, economics or other appropriate subject. *Applicants do not need to have any specialised knowledge of the Social Security scheme.*

"It's all so academic," said Mary.

"All so far away," I said. "All I need is a little allowance, no matter how small so long as it is regular, so that I could budget and be left in peace. No going out looking for snoopers on the corner like a criminal on the run. No fear of someone coming to tell me that as from next Monday my allowance will be stopped for some reason I've never heard of."

Poverty is a real and tangible thing. The old people were right when they taught us "When poverty walks in through the door love flies out of the window". He did enter the door and his great shape blotted out every other thing. He ruled our lives. We could not go out but he'd whisper, "Can you afford it? The bus fare is a shilling." He'd even accompany me on the bus and say, "Try to avoid paying. Then you'll have enough to buy supper."

He made our tempers short and our nerves frayed. He turned a simple breakage of a small household item into a great tragedy. He kept us away from any social activities, he did his best to make me slatternly and uncaring. He tried his hardest to push me right down and give up even thinking.

Had there been an allowance, however small, I could have kept him chained in a corner. As it was, with our income changing and fluctuating, never knowing when some official would come and tell us YOU CAN'T HAVE ANY MORE OFF THE STATE, he became a great shapeless monster. He was torture, forcing me slowly to give in to him completely, to sink . . .

It was months before Mervyn could start working again. The works superintendent had visited him in hospital and told him his job would be kept open for him, for he and his staff had been shocked at his illness—and his efforts to start work. His kindness helped to save Mervyn's life. Later, I saw some of the men he'd worked with on the day he'd been there. They had been horrified.

"He couldn't work," they told me. "He just stood there

shivering the whole day long. He was so cold. We knew he was very ill but he wouldn't go home." They were very good to him, these men, for he wasn't fit to work. Not now. But as soon as his doctor gave his permission he trudged off each morning, part-time because of his damaged lungs, losing days every week because of the epilepsy.

An S.S. officer came up immediately and told me I'd have to go to work.

The health visitor said I could not possibly work with Mervyn in his present state. I must be at home to look after him. He needed hot meals when he came in; he was, she said, still a part-invalid, lucky to be alive. She went in to fight the S.S. officers, with the backing of the health department and doctors, and won a victory. I was to stay at home.

Phil was in the lower sixth now at the grammar school, and had to have a different blazer, which admittedly beautiful garment cost £8. Away with false pride, I said with an air, and applied to the council education welfare department for a grant for his clothes, and here I was met with such kindness that I was amazed; they were actually *willing* to help, and didn't want to fight about it, or say we didn't deserve it and why didn't I go to work and why hadn't I any insurance stamps. Charity was a little warmer here.

But Phil's new blazer, however welcome, was but a drop in the ocean. I found I was still not getting enough to live on.

Mervyn's wage was, I think, the lowest in the country for men. His job consisted of picking up waste paper in the parks and town in summer and shovelling snow in winter, not ideal work, but there was little else he could do then. He was still of high intelligence, but the drugs made him slow and he could not work a full week. Certainly no other employer would look at him. My own Social Security payments, low in the first place, were made lower for two reasons: I always had to find the full mortgage repayments, and I had to buy my insurance stamp—when I could, that is (and if I wanted an old age pension; I could have applied for non-payment and lived on Social Security for life). As time went on I found I owed £50 in stamps.

I am not a bad manager, or a scrounger, or careless with money, or a spendthrift, but I state here categorically that it is impossible to life for more than a short time on National Assistance. It is generally recognised now that pensions are too low for old people. How much worse, then, for the young, who eat so much, and who need so many more clothes.

Having such a low income for a long period meant that nothing in the house could be replaced, and there seemed no point in bashing my head at the brick wall of Security only to be told "no". The carpets, nearly twenty years old, were in holes. The dining chairs kept falling apart—dangerous if you happened to be sitting on them—while I prayed every night that the fence wouldn't blow down and nothing in the house would break. Then in the space of a fortnight, by that law of averages which every housewife knows, everything did break.

The vacuum cleaner, also twenty years old, gave up the ghost, and I asked about getting it repaired but the man said it was too old, they couldn't get the parts, so I had to go back to brush and shovel. The washing machine packed in, and the nearest launderette was a good mile away. My sheets suddenly showed gaping holes, all of them, and our one lavatory refused to function, so we had to pour down buckets of water.

So, I thought, if I hadn't enough to live on, dammit, I'd find enough. I started writing in the few hours Mervyn was at work. Somehow I'd keep the home together, maybe in time I'd earn enough to be free. I had forgotten that to Social Security it is a sin to help yourself. In the name of not making you too comfortable on the worthy insurance payers' taxes, you are encouraged to stay at the bottom for life. I always thought it would be cheaper for everyone, including the worthy tax payers, to help someone get on their feet and support themselves, but maybe I had odd thoughts.

So, with the goal of supporting myself and poor Mervyn, I began to earn. Not much at first, and I was allowed to earn £2. I bought a second-hand vacuum cleaner, and thought of all the time wasted asking for discretionary benefits always refused, so carried on earning enough to buy a new chair or two, have the lavatory repaired and buy some of the most urgent necessities. I sent my returns to the income tax office very honestly, deducting my expenses. I was determined that Mervyn should not go back to hospital.

I wrote articles for the local paper under my own name, and I hit out gaily at bureaucracy. The town laughed. I don't know what bureaucracy thought. As I saw it, I was saving the country money; if I had all the things I was, according to the Supplementary Benefits Handbook, entitled to, I should have been paid more from the tax-paying public than by earning it myself. And it was much less wearing to earn myself than to try to squeeze a drop of milk of human kindness out of the Social Security stone. No doubt, I philosophised as I did my ironing, no doubt it isn't the country's place to pay to look after a woman's kids.

"G.B.S.," Mary told me, "said that if a widow has children, borne at great cost to herself in pain, danger and disablement, the children do not belong to her in any real or legal sense. When she has reared them they pass from her into the community as independent persons, marrying strangers, working for strangers, spending on the community the life that has been built up at her expense. No more monstrous injustice could be imagined than that the burden of rearing the children should fall on her alone and not on the celibate and the selfish as well."

"I'm not a widow," I said.

"No, but in Shaw's day, don't you see, widows were treated much as divorcees are now. Poor ones, that is. My mother could remember seeing them send their kids to the workhouse to fetch 'charity bread', while their little pals called 'charity kids' after them. The Victorian bourgeoisie identified goodness with thrift and making money. It was sinful to be poor, and this attitude lingers."

"What a pity the Church doesn't preach Christianity," I said. "About the rich being doomed to damnation and the poor being blessed."

"Yes, well," said Mary. "Then you had to feel guilty if you were poor, now you have to feel guilty if you're divorced. Look at all this stuff written about broken homes and the juvenile delinquents who come from these establishments— poor ones, of course."

"After my experience I'm surprised any such children ever grow up to be honest citizens," I commented. "But they do. Mine did."

"Except that Phil's going to blow up the Houses of Parliament or something."

"True. I wonder if anyone has done a survey into the backgrounds of these militant students," I pondered. "Were they poor, too? Or discriminated against?"

For although we have a law about not discriminating against colour, and women are asking for one about sex, no one notices that fatherless children are discriminated against by the State.

Margaret Wynn writes in *Fatherless Families*: "A child is insured through his payments to the State under National Insurance against the sickness of his father, against the unemployment of his father, against the death of his father while still in the family circle and against the loss of both his parents. But in one important aspect the child remains uncovered, he is not insured against the loss of his father by desertion, separation or divorce, although the estimates show this is one of the gravest and most considerable risks which the child faces ... A child may receive more support from the State after his father's death than the State was able to secure for him in his father's life-time."

Even after the father's death the child is still discriminated against, various differing rates being paid depending on how the father died. Was he killed in the armed forces? From industrial injury or disease? Or did he just die at home? Was he married or separated? Divorced? Did he maintain the child or not? Was the child living with his father? If he is illegitimate yet living with mother and stepfather he may get nothing, while his stepbrothers will. And so on.

Writes Margaret Wynn: "The Social insurance still leaves some children less privileged than others for no good reason and leaves some children totally unprovided for. It is a curious feature of the present law that it results in foster parents being altogether better treated than the mothers of fatherless children. In some cases the strain of living on such a low income has the effect of breaking up the fatherless family altogether and transferring the care of the child to a local authority and then to a foster parent."

She goes on to compare child allowances in other countries.

"In Denmark the total expense of maintaining a child in a good foster home is the 'standard contribution' on which benefits to all fatherless children are based.

"In Australia and New Zealand class A widows' pensions are given to widowed mothers and their children and also to fatherless families at the same rate. For Class A, the term widow includes a deserted wife, a divorcee, a woman whose husband is in prison or a mental hospital. The child under Australian and New Zealand law is insured against desertion by his father and against failure of the father to support him during the father's lifetime as well as against his death. The unsupported mother is recognised. Both countries are far ahead of Great Britain.

"In France Family Allowances are paid for the second and later children, but they continue later than in Britain for students. An extra allowance is paid to families where there is only one bread-winner in addition.

"In Sweden, Belgium and Holland, the Family Allowance is paid for all first children, and in Norway it is paid for the first child of an only parent.

"When a marriage breaks up the wife and children in Britain are not covered by National Insurance. They have the right at civil law to be maintained by the husband and father, but there remain many difficulties for the mother in obtaining the regular payment of her maintenance money. Should the father disappear there is little she can do.

"When the Royal Commission on Marriage and Divorce produced its report in 1956, many suggestions had been put forward that Government departments should help the wife by giving her husband's address in order that she could sue for maintenance. The Commission rejected these proposals, saying, 'Against the right of a wife to maintenance must be balanced the right of the husband to have his privacy respected, in our view the latter must prevail'." (Repeated in 1971.)

Legislation may be passed to amend this, but somehow legislation never seems to make much difference. At least, it didn't to me. There are always ways to slip around the law.

But Mervyn continued to work, and I gave him the best food. Gradually his strength returned, as much as it ever would with less than one lung. He was more cheerful, too. He so desperately wanted to be an ordinary member of the community, earning his living. Maybe he was wrong, in this day and age. But Mervyn was the sort of person our civilised pecking order pushes to the end of every queue. He was truthful, good, gentle, and so honest as to be painful. He obeyed all the commandments, he loved his neighbour, he was a much better person than I'll ever be. And it was precisely these Christian qualities which, together with the epilepsy, made him an outsider.

Spring came to Hicktown, always a great event. Our

winters were hard and we were unprotected from the cold
and the damp. Only a few houses had central heating and
many still burned coal. So when the slush and the ice and the
fog changed into the soft winds full of birds' cries, and crocuses
and daffodils took the winds of March with beauty, we were
overjoyed as the pagans of old. The gaunt black skeletons of
trees in Perronporth Road were suddenly pale green with new
pulsing life, forsythia flamed, almond and cherry were great
masses of blossom, and we saluted the resurrection of the
world.

We were happy that spring and summer of 1969. Mervyn
still lost much time from work, but he felt he was taking one
step towards normality, towards being self-sufficient. He began
to join clubs in the town, went to classes at Tech.

Kay was going to London, where she would stay with a
friend. She'd be over regularly, she said. But she was growing
up, I realised, she was attractive, she would marry.

Phil had found a job with a small grocer's at weekends,
where he earned several shillings to provide himself with the
pocket money I couldn't give him. I did not mention this fact
to the S.S. people, knowing it would be stopped from my
allowance. Phil told me not to worry about my insurance
stamps. "When I have a good job I'll look after you," he
promised.

I was surprised they didn't find out about the greengrocer.
For often, when I went to the butcher's next door to it, Officer
Two would be in there. And often Officer Three would be
sitting on the corner in her car. Perhaps she had nothing to
do, I mused, or perhaps all the rest of the residential estate
lived on Social Security. I didn't know, for I never told anyone except Mary that I lived on it; it was a shameful secret
which you kept to yourself. If anyone asked me how I made a
living I said by writing, and never once thought about
snoopers.

Then Officer Three called and told me that I must register
for work. She'd had orders from area office, who I'm sure had
me pigeon-holed as work-shy. I asked what about Mervyn.
She replied that the registering was merely a formality, that I
wouldn't have to go to work really, I'd still be paid, and she'd
see them personally in the labour exchange to tell them. Trust-
ing as ever, I went down.

Supplementary Benefits Handbook, Para. 6–8: *"The*

*Commission have power to decide that payment of supple-
mentary allowance shall be subject to the condition that the
person registers for work at an Employment Exchange of the
Department of Employment and Productivity. This rule is
normally applied to anyone who is capable of work. For
certain groups of people the requirement to register may be
waived or registration for part-time work only may be required, depending on all the circumstances of the case; these
include (1) People required at home to care for sick relatives,
(2) Women widowed in later middle life with no experience
in the employment field."*

Para. 132 : *"A woman of working age who has to stay off
work to care for a sick or aged relative may be awarded a
supplementary allowance without being required to register
for employment."*

At the labour exchange I saw a pleasant young lady, who
listened to my story with some amazement, as well she might.
No, she had heard nothing from Social Security, but then, she
whispered confidentially, they're an odd lot in there.

I brightened. "You can say that again," I said. "So what
do I do?"

"Well, can you work at all?"

I pondered. "I might manage part-time. I have to get
Mervyn's meals, you see, he finishes at four. This is for the
T.B. But the real problem is the epilepsy. When he has attacks
I must be at home, and this means practically one or two
days a week. No employer is going to take me on those terms,
and if I don't tell him—"

"You'd get the sack," she finished. "Well, I think the best
thing to do is to get a doctor's certificate saying you can work
part-time, and we'll send it to the city."

"What for?" I asked in astonishment.

"To get permission for you to work part-time. I don't know
whether it will be granted. We can but try."

"Our red tape must cost the country an awful lot in
stamps," I said. "But in the meantime do I get unemployment benefit?"

"Oh no, your benefit has run out, you see."

"So what do I get?"

"You'll get Social Security, but they'll bring it in here and
we'll pay it to you."

"How nice," I said, politely.

"And there is one other difference. You can only earn £1 now instead of £2."

I made an appointment to see my doctor, and he gave me a certificate. This was a different doctor from the first one who'd given me a certificate; this made two doctors, plus the health department's doctors, all sending certificates to Social Security. I told the health visitor of the latest development. She said *of course* I could not possibly work more than part-time, and would I tell the S.S. people to ring the M.o.H.'s department, and *he* would tell them too.

I said, "We're fighting a losing battle, you know." She patted my shoulder and went out.

The doctor's certificate was sent to the city and I awaited results. In time a letter came marked importantly : "Insurance Officer's Decision. 21st April 1969.

"Unemployment benefit is not payable for the period 5.4.69 to 18.4.69 (both dates included) because there is no reasonable prospect of the claimant's securing employment owing to the restrictions she has placed on the conditions of employment she is prepared to accept, and she has not shown that these restrictions are reasonable :

(1) having regard to all the circumstances and that they would not prevent her from having reasonable prospects of obtaining employment but for temporary adverse industrial conditions, or

(2) in view of her physical condition, or

(3) having regard to the nature of her usual occupation and the time she has been employed.

The National Insurance (Unemployment and Sickness Benefit Regulations.)

"Note : A similar decision will be given on any claim for later days on which the circumstances remain unchanged.

"Yours faithfully,

"Department of Employment and Productivity.

"If you wish to appeal to the local tribunal against the Insurance Officer's decision and will let me know, I will send you a form on which to make your appeal. As there is a time limit for making an appeal, the completed form should reach this office within 21 days from the date of this letter."

"This may surprise you," I said to the pleasant girl, "but I have no faith in tribunals."

She smiled faintly. "If it had been your own health that

was bad," she said, "you could have been granted the decision."

"So what do I do now?"

"Tell the Security people, they'll have to pay you again."

I reported back, and was told that I couldn't claim any more unless I registered for work because my son Phil was seventeen.

"But he's still at school," I said, amazed. They were adamant. No more Security payment for Mrs Colin. By order.

I decided to see the manager, but had no idea how to see this obviously imposing being. His name came on a rubber stamp on all my letters, true, but he never had answered any of the letters I wrote to him asking him so many questions about how his department worked. But there had to be a manager. I reasoned, and rang to make an appointment. He wasn't in, I was told.

Next day I rang again. He was having lunch, or tea, or signing things in triplicate; he could never see me.

I wrote to him, marking the letter private and confidential, asking to make an appointment. The letter was not answered.

I rang again. The telephonist asked my name. I refused to give it. She slammed down the phone.

"Looking around corners for you," I sang, and went down to the S.S. offices and waited my turn to see the granite-faced receptionist. "Yes?" she asked, without looking up.

I said, "I'd like to make an appointment to see the manager."

She looked up now, recognition dawning in her eyes. Here was the potential spanner in the works approaching. She said, without batting an eyelid, "You'll have to write to make an appointment."

"Good God, woman," I exploded, losing my temper as I always do, no matter how many times I say I won't, that this time I'll be patient, that they are human beings too . . . "Good God, I've written and phoned."

"If you write," she said, calmly, "and address the letter to the manager, of course it just comes into the general office."

"Oh, does it, begod?" I asked. "Now I know why the letters were never answered. But I marked that last one private. Doesn't that mean anything to you?"

"If you write a personal letter to the Manager you should mark it 'For the attention of Mr Burro-Crat'," she said.

"And in triplicate?" I asked, sweetly.

She glared, and I glared, and then I went home and wrote a letter marking it For the Attention of Mr Burro-Crat. But nothing happened.

Persistence is my middle name, and I was determined to see the manager. If he lived I'd see him. I rang daily. He was always out.

But one lucky day I managed to get hold of the Nice Man. I knew it was him, for as soon as I said, "Hello," he said, "Hello, Mrs Colin."

"You know me?" I asked. Though it would be difficult to say who didn't know me at his establishment.

"Your dog bit me," he said, simply. And when I asked about an appointment he said, "Yes, of course. When would you like to come?" I went the next afternoon.

In the event Mr Burro-Crat was a very pleasant man, who listened courteously to my story, and said he would look into it and would I call again when he had done this. He'd let me know.

I didn't expect to hear another word, but in a few days the letter came fixing another appointment. "One should never deal with underlings," I said as I set out.

When I went into his office the manager was sitting with Officer Five, who had my file open on his knees.

I did most of the talking. The manager said that, as Phil was seventeen, I must register for work.

I asked why, when he was still at school. Before he could tell me it was the law, or orders from area office, I said, "A widow doesn't have to work if she has children under nineteen. Why should my children be treated differently?", and this nonplussed him for a moment.

He said something about husband's insurance stamps. "But my husband paid insurance stamps," I flashed. "And for that matter still pays them, which a widow's husband can't very well. So why shouldn't my children, whose father is still paying taxes, be treated the same as a widow's, whose husband may have stopped paying years and years ago?"

There was no answer to that, of course. Except that I suddenly remembered that it wasn't for Phil I was having to stay at home but for Mervyn, and I told him this.

"But Mervyn is working," he said.

I sighed. I had told them the position so many times, the

doctors had told them, the health department had told them. Mervyn wasn't fit to work at all, he tried . . . but on the days when he was ill I had to be at home with him. Couldn't they judge a case on its merits just once? Just for the novelty?

For the irony of it all was that if Mervyn hadn't tried, if he'd been too lazy to work, if he'd been a scrounger, they'd have paid him happily, and paid me too, to look after him. This, to me, is the crux of the whole stupid Social Security system, that you are penalised if you *try*.

This is where our present system is even more backward than the old workhouse one. The former system was to humiliate the pauper so much that he would get out and find work. Today the humiliation part still stands, and you're not only humiliated, but prosecuted if you try to help yourself. It is thus impossible to rise. If I keep stressing this point it is because it strikes me as so odd as to be utterly incomprehensible. Mervyn wanted to work, I wanted to work; his health made it impossible for us to earn enough to live on. All we needed was a little *extra* so that Mervyn could work *when* he could and thus retain his self-respect, and by retaining his self-respect be a better human being, when his health would improve and maybe we'd eventually become self-supporting and save the country money . . .

Officer Five said, "You have been earning money by writing."

"I have." I had made no secret of it, ever—even now my name was over an article in our local paper. I had nothing to hide. I was earning money for my family, and I was not ashamed of it.

Officer Five mentioned another magazine which had published some of my outpourings. I raised my eyebrows. Nice work, special investigators. For this was a woman's magazine.

He asked if I'd give permission for them to write round and ask everyone how much I'd earned. Suppose I said no, I wondered. Would they write to everyone they could think of? *Every newspaper and publication in the country to check if Jean Colin had been earning money?* What a lot of stamps. And they'd do it too, to save the tax-payer money. Didn't they realise that if I hadn't been honest I could just have written under another name?

I wasn't terribly sold on the idea of letting all would-be employers know I was suspected of diddling Social Security. I was just a beginner at writing after all. So I said no, and we compromised on my agreeing to bring down all receipts from payments received.

"Wait a minute," I said. "It isn't all profit. I have expenses. Paper, envelopes, stamps . . ."

I took my receipts down to Officer Five together with a list of my expenses, but he said he would not allow me as many expenses as the inland revenue. Nor did he allow me an insurance stamp. There was their own little rule, which was, as always for Social Security, just a little more grudging than any other government department, just to remind you that you were living off the country.

Officer Five said he would let me earn £4 a week from now on, and I nearly fell off my chair in surprise. Was I really going to be helped to stand on my own feet?

That's what comes of seeing the manager, I thought, gleefully.

When I sent my year's returns to the inland revenue my taxable income was £250, just a little less than £5 a week: £4 a week which I was allowed to earn, plus an insurance stamp which I allowed myself to earn. If I'd employed an accountant he would have reduced this to a loss in no time. (I've typed accounts since then.)

One odd little point I could never understand about Social Security was that my earnings had to be totalled over the year and then divided into average weekly earnings. I could not, say, earn £20 in one week, stop the Social Security for that week, then carry on. Yet if I'd gone to a job and earned £250 in six weeks I could then have drawn Social Security payments for the rest of the year. Spreading it over the year meant that I always lost on the deal. I asked why this should be, but no one seemed to know. Or if they did they weren't telling.

Later I was given my allowance book back and told that, when I had been living on Assistance for two years, I should not have the extra 10s. allowable for long-term endurance, as my long run had been broken by the visit to the labour exchange. But it didn't matter, I shouldn't have had it anyway, as I already had the additional 10s. for extra food for ex-T.B. patients.

THE END

"We worry about our dogs, cats and pigeons; we pour out aid
for the hungry and helpless overseas; we search our consciences
endlessly about the treatment of criminals and try to deal with
them humanely. But our disabled we throw on the scrap heap."
—*Nursing Times*

P H I L W A S I N the throes of his A-levels. It had been a
long, hard summer for him, and indeed for all other examinees.
But we thought the end justified the effort; if we had to
choose between the rat-race and poverty it would be the rat-
race every time. So Phil worked, and studied, and worked.
He read economics and social history and was interested in
changing the world. He knew what needed changing,
especially at home.

I was feeling fairly placid. Worried as always about the
future I had, in January, asked how much I should get when
Phil left school. As he was eighteen now his payment had
jumped up to £3 5s. od., and Officer Two told me that this
would be stopped; but as long as I provided medical certificates saying that I had to stay at home to look after Mervyn
I should get the remainder—£6 18s. od. It wouldn't be much,
but I'd manage if I earned a little, and Mervyn paid for his
keep.

My father, at this time, was living alone, and was growing
increasingly feeble. His house was too small for us to join him,
and mine was too small for him to join us. I wasn't quite sure
how I'd manage if he should come to be bedridden for a long
time, but I figured out that somehow I'd do it, provided I
had my small allowances. We visited him as often as we could,
especially Mervyn, who had always been the apple of his eye.

June came, and the sun shone occasionally, as the sun does
in England. My garden was having a good year; pansies
bloomed, and the clematis, with its blackbird's nest, was in
full bloom. I had roses, pinks, violets and honeysuckle. Even

the sweet-peas made an effort and gave us a fine showing of multi-coloured flowers.

Officer Three called.

"When is Phil leaving school?" she asked abruptly.

I hadn't thought past his exams. "Why, at the end of term, I suppose," I said.

"Not so," said the officer. "He leaves now, when his exams are finished." (She knew when they'd end, I didn't.) "He must go down to the labour exchange immediately and register for employment, and he'll get his own payment, and may I have your book, please?"

Dumbfounded, I gave it to her, and dumbly watched her go. I didn't tell Phil for a week, until he had quite done, and was preparing to relax and get a hard-earned rest. Then I broke the news.

He sighed. Phil is a boy of few words. He was the lean and hungry type, he thought much. Doubtless the official mind would think it quite silly anyway. Why should a boy object to having to run down to the labour exchange to claim Social Security?

Phil still said nothing. He found his own job for the holidays.

I said, "I'm sorry, Phil."

There are these little griefs in being poor. I remember when the chimney sweep came and, while working, told me proudly that his son had passed for Cambridge, and so he'd bought him a record-player. I was so pleased at this success, for it was something that would never have happened pre-war. But I wished that, just once, I could have bought my children expensive presents.

Phil said, "It's all right, all the boys do it, you know."

I did know, but most of them packed it in when they'd had enough, or when they were going away for a few weeks by the sea. They wouldn't have to slog away till the day before they went to college; no rest at all. I studied Phil's thin frame nervously.

Kay had gone to London. She had talked to me about it, asking if she were letting me down, saying she felt guilty, but I stopped her. "No guilt," I said, firmly. "Leave the guilt where it belongs—with me."

"Not at all," said my darling daughter, grandly. "You and father were incompatible, that's all. There was nothing more you could have done."

Cheering words from one who, according to all the books, should have been a delinquent. Even more cheering were those she said to a friend of hers, just divorced and feeling guilty and a failure. "Look at me," said my sweet daughter. "My mother brought three of us up on her own, and I'm fine."

She went to London, and wrote home ecstatically that the pay there was out of this world, that she was praised as a very good worker, and employers liked the way she worked so hard (she'd had good training); that she was going to evening classes to study shorthand, O-levels and Spanish. All this cost money, but Kay was making out. "Everything's so different here," she ended. "No one has any idea what life in Hicktown is like."

Phil grunted as I read that last sentence to him. He'd soon be away. Mervyn and I would find it hard going alone, but I pinned my faith on making enough to support myself in a year or two's time. I had nothing else to do but work; with Phil gone I'd find it difficult to get out to shop on bad days when Mervyn would be ill the whole time and could not be left. But I wanted Phil to go. I wasn't too worried about my payments. After all, I had been told I'd get £6 18s. od. I waited for my book.

I had a letter from the Social Security dated 9th July 1970.

"You will recall that when you and I discussed your supplementary allowance last year I informed you that the whole position would need to be reviewed when Phil left school. As this event has now taken place the whole question of the amount and method of payment needs to be reappraised.

"I think the best way to go about this is for you to call on me here, and I suggest that Wednesday, 15th July, at 10.30 a.m., would be a suitable time.

"In the meantime I am enclosing a giro order for your payment for week commencing 13th July 1970.

"Yours faithfully,
"Department of Social Security."

The giro payment for the week was £5.

The sun shone on the flowers, and on the tatty furniture and the threadbare carpets. I picked up a newspaper: "Average earnings of Britain's adult males in full-time manual work were £26 16s. od. last April, according to statistics published in the Employment and Productivity Gazette.

Women manual workers were about £13 8s. od. Non-manual workers did much better. Men's average earnings were £35 16s. od. a week, with a tenth getting more than £55. Woman non-manual workers averaged £17 16s. od."

Inflation was rampant, prices were going sky-high. Mortgage rates went up and up, as did everything else. There was still so much I needed in the house, and I'd had no new clothes for years. We had a roof over our heads, true, and we had food, for I put that second after I'd paid the mortgage and the rates and the electricity and the gas.

I looked at the giro payment. I'd been thinking I'd get £7, had been budgeting for this ... I'd maybe have managed as long as I earned a little and Mervyn paid out most of his poor wages ... Rage suddenly swamped me, that he, who had so little, should have to give up so much.

Five-pounds for not working. For looking after a sick son who could not carry on without my help, for which I was treated as some sort of criminal.

Rebellion was working in me, rebellion that had been passed down through God knows how many generations. I sent back the £5. I had long dreamed of the day when I should be well-off enough to tell Them what to do with the money they doled out so grudgingly. Now I found I couldn't wait that long. But I merely said, first, that I could not live on £5 a week as my household expenses, before food and clothing, were £8.

I went to the office of Social Security as commanded. Kay came over and went with me. Kay is a bonny fighter. We went through the public entrance of the Social Security where the usual drab people waited for attendance, and were ushered into the inner sanctum.

"Follow me," said Officer Five.

"To Room 101 ?" I said.

"I beg your pardon?"

"Just a touch of whimsy."

We entered a pleasant little office, with a carpet and venetian blinds and a large desk. The officer was friendly and smiling. He introduced a girl who sat at the side. She, he said, was an authority on welfare.

He said I should now go to work.

I looked at him speechlessly. This was where I had come in. Wearily I pointed out my problems, as I had pointed them out so many times, as the health department and doctors had pointed them out. I could not work because Mervyn lost so much time.

He said, "I have a list of the number of times Mervyn has been absent from his job in the past few months. He had very few days off."

I did not ask him from where he obtained his information. I only knew that wherever it was from, it was wrong. I mentioned that Mervyn had just been off for a fortnight with flu.

"We don't count that," said the officer.

I was outside the rules again, for I counted it. So did his doctor, who'd been just a bit worried about those high temperatures . . . But I didn't argue.

The officer said that, however, if I obtained a medical certificate this might be overcome. I asked, "Don't you remember last year? Those certificates still apply. Mervyn hasn't suddenly grown another lung, or stopped being epileptic." *Would that he had.*

He said, "There is your writing."

There was indeed. My unashamed efforts to maintain my family, keep a home fire burning, so *wrong* . . . I said, "You allowed me to earn £4 a week, remember?"

"Oh no," he replied, "that was only for a few weeks."

"You never told me that," I said. They still had the power to amaze me. Had I been earning too much money? "Do you want to prosecute me?" I asked. "Maybe it would be a good thing, bring it all into the open."

He said, "I have on your file the amounts you told me you earned last time you were here."

"Yes?" What now? What was I supposed to do, make a forced confession? *I have been earning £4 a week which I shouldn't have, although I didn't know I shouldn't have* . . . I remembered fleetingly that I'd read how the Birmingham Claimants' Union advised their members to take a tape-recorder with them to Social Security interviews . . .

The officer said, "Before I grant you any more aid I shall have to write to every firm you've written for. Or you can't have any more money."

I sighed. "Supposing I let you do this?" I asked. *Let everyone know, what's it matter?* "Supposing I get more medical certificates, how much shall I be granted then to keep my home going and look after my son?"

He said, "£5. And you could earn £1."

That finished me. I couldn't live on £5 unless I earned more than £1. Could anyone, when they paid £8 a week for mortgage repayments, rates, heating, light, food? And if I couldn't earn more than £1, there wasn't much point in asking employers what I'd earned from writing, for there wouldn't be any more writing.

I said, "You realise that this means I can't carry on?"

There was no reply.

I asked the welfare expert for her advice. The officer said she wasn't a welfare expert.

This wasn't *1984*, it was *Alice in Wonderland*.

And then I let logic and reason go by the board, and blamed the officer for everything the civil service had ever done or will ever do. I blamed him for all the red tape that had ever been tied around human efforts, all the rule-books that wouldn't let you live, merely kept you existing, all the secrecy, the snooping... I saw bureaucracy personified in Officer Five, and I said everything I'd been longing to say for two years. If I hadn't been so angry I'd have felt sorry for the officer, for it wasn't his fault, but it is an occupational hazard of Social Security that its employees risk fierce onslaughts. Perhaps they should get danger money. Kay added a speech of her own, while the welfare officer who wasn't cowered in a corner.

"You haven't beaten me," I fired as a parting shot. "Nor Mervyn, either, because you will never break our spirit. That's something no one can ever do, anywhere, in any country, however hard they try. I'm not sorry for myself, I'm sorry for you, because I'd never do your job, never. And you know it." Then we swept out, penniless but defiant.

I went home and my exhilaration evaporated. We had no money. I was finished. If I couldn't earn more than £1 I couldn't go on, and writing was a chancy business at best; there were no part-time jobs in Hicktown, and unemployment was growing. Never any temporary jobs as in cities. I could not take in boarders because of Mervyn's attacks; people didn't like them, and our house was open-plan. I couldn't buy another house because I wouldn't get a mortgage at my age and with no income. If the health department found us a council house, as I'm sure they would, there'd be such a carry-on with the S.S. about paying the rent... *You can't expect the country to pay your rent, Mrs Colin...* I couldn't live on £5 a week, but in a council house, rent paid, if I earned more than £1 in any one week then bang would go my Security rent . . . No, I couldn't face any more of that, I'd had as much as I could take.

There was nothing to do but put the house up for sale and Mervyn in a home.

And I knew then I couldn't stand Hicktown any longer. That if I stayed I'd forget the officer was a respectable Social Security man and think that he, and all the others, had a grudge against me

I wrote to the British Epilepsy Society, who said Mervyn could be admitted to a colony only through the welfare department. I went to the health department. Everyone was on holiday. I hadn't seen a welfare officer for two years.

I rang every few days. Wrote letters. At last I found someone to talk to. I was told that they didn't believe in handicapped people being sent away from home. I said I didn't either. Keep invalids at home. I'd seen them and their families during my visits to Social Security. Community care. Family care, they really mean, and family care means one person being worked into a nervous breakdown or an early grave, all in the sacred name of motherhood.

I pointed out that I had no money. This they didn't seem to grasp. I said family care is fine if you have money, and I spelled it out . . . I have no money . . . *no money* . . . NO MONEY . . . No, I couldn't get help from Social Security . . . not enough to live on . . . Not enough for a house heavily mortgaged which I had thought was going to be a home for the family . . . Now none of us will have a home . . . That's where the theories get us, the statistics and social administration and the Welfare State—to a hundred thousand children coming into care, nearly all of whom are children without two parents, and who cost the country £20,000,000 a year. So many broken homes . . . Break this one too . . .

How much will it cost the county council to pay for Mervyn in a home? If I'd had one tenth of that I could have given him family care, kept the house going, our home . . . Now he'll have nowhere . . . But thank you, you can't help it, it isn't your department, God knows you've tried . . . No, I don't want you to ask them for more on my behalf, not again . . . not for another six months or so and then have it all start again . . . Just forgive me if I'm bitter . . . Goodbye.

There were genuine regrets. The family breaking up, the house going. Guilt poured over me, making me want to weep. *But what had I done?* Did I have to be punished for ever for being poor? Even criminals didn't have life sentences now. Gypsy padded round the house uneasily, knowing something was wrong, even she could not comfort me. They'll miss you, Gypsy . . . And that poor old man sitting bowed in his chair, is this all he gets for a lifetime's hard work?

I had no income from June to the following January 1971, when the house was sold. I pondered going to my M.P. again, but I knew I just couldn't take any more fighting for existence. I felt numb; later on the pain would start.

I paid off my debts, and suddenly knew a feeling of overwhelming relief. No longer would I have to tote that weary load, trying to keep a house going in face of rampant inflation. I had been a slave too long. No more tatty threadbare carpet, no more praying that the washing machine wouldn't break down, no more feeling guilty at owning a washing machine at all. No more lying awake listening to hear if the wind was blowing the fence down. No more nailing the chairs/wardrobe/sideboard together . . . No more poverty.

Poverty is not relative, as our social worker friend tells us from her home in St John's Wood. Poverty is not ennobling, as the clergy would have us believe. Poverty is mean and petty, and puts one in the power of mean, petty people. It is a slow wearing of the nerves till there is nothing left but either acceptance and servility or fighting and going mad. I was getting out in time. Just.

We all crammed into my father's little house, and immediately his supplementary pension was stopped and his home help. So we had to move out again, and my father was left alone till he collapsed and the neighbours had to break a window to get in.

Phil went to college on a grant more than twice as much as I had been given for him. Kay was working hard. They'd be all right. I couldn't bear to think of Mervyn, the gentle, who loved "birds and green places and the wind on the heath, and saw the brightness of the skirts of God", who treated the world gently, and found in return that it rended him like a ravening wolf. Tore him in little pieces in the name of the Welfare State.

I went to take one last look at the garden where I'd worked

so hard. Indian summer, and the clematis still bloomed, the blackbirds were coming again. The sun shone in mellow glory over the pansies and the honeysuckle and the sweet peas. It was a beautiful world.

It was an unhappy world with so much ugliness and pain and poverty, and man's inhumanity to man, all hidden by careful fiction about nice people with nice manners who read comfortable statistics that the country is so nice. It was an improving world because so many of the young were casting off the old hypocrisies and being honest about selfishness and greed and incompetence. Bliss is it in this dawn to be alive and to be young is very heaven.

Gypsy and I set out alone, two middle-aged drop-outs— maybe it would be truer to say we'd been dropped out—two who'd tried and failed. We did not look back and our heads were still high.

But I had to leave Gypsy with strangers while I went away to earn my living. Six months later she died.

The vet said it was her heart.

Broken.

BIBLIOGRAPHY

The Yorkist Age by Paul Murray Kendall (Allen & Unwin, 1962).

The Mothers by Robert Briffault (Allen & Unwin, 1959).

The Inside of Divorce by Bill Mortlock (Constable, 1972).

Marriage at Risk by Michael Benson (Peter Davies, 1958).

Fatherless Families by Margaret Wynn (Michael Joseph, 1964).

Bulletins of Married Women's Association.

Social and Economic History of England by Pauline Gregg (George G. Harrap & Co, 1964).

The English Legal System by Radcliffe & Cross (Butterworth, 1964).

First Book of English Law by O. Hood Phillips (Sweet & Maxwell, 1965).

Report of the National Assistance Board, 1965.

Supplementary Benefits Handbook, 1970.

Preface to *Misalliance* by George Bernard Shaw (Constable, 1910).

Sex in Society by Alex Comfort (Gerald Duckworth & Co, 1963).

Tribunals in the Social Services by Kathleen Bell (Routledge and Kegan Paul, 1969).

The Roads to Ruin by E. S. Turner (Michael Joseph, 1950).